****

GARDENING HANDBOOK

Newly Revised

by T. H. Everett

A FAWCETT GOLD MEDAL BOOK
Fawcett Publications, Inc., Greenwich, Conn.
Member of American Book Publishers Council, Inc.

Cover photo by Malak, Freelance Photographers Guild

Unless otherwise credited, photographs in this book are by T. H. Everett.

Illustrations are by Miss Tabea Hofmann and Frank Schwarz.

Printed in the United States of America

About the Author

With a professional gardening career going back to 1916, T. H. Everett is eminently qualified to write authoritatively on the pleasures and problems, ways and means of the home gardener. He is well-known as a writer and lecturer on horticultural subjects, a teacher of gardening, and a gardening columnist.

Mr. Everett was born in Lancashire, England, and obtained his early professional training in some of the finest gardens of that country. Before coming to the United States in 1927, he was graduated from the School of Gardening of the Royal Botanic Garden, Kew, near London, receiving the National Diploma in Horticulture from the Royal Horticultural Society.

In 1932 Mr. Everett was appointed Horticulturist at The New York Botanical Garden. For more than thirty years he administered the horticultural development and maintenance there of one of the best-known gardens and one of the largest collections of living plants in America, and directed an extensive educational program of instruction in gardening, landscape gardening, botany, nature study, and allied fields. He now serves the Garden as Senior Horticulture Specialist.

Mr. Everett is the author of several books and pocket guides on flowers and gardening and the editor of the *New Illustrated Encyclopedia of Gardening*.

Contents

GARDENING HANDBOOK

Your Garden Plan

❋❋

In creating a new garden, no matter how small it is to be, plan it first on paper and draw it to scale. But before you put pencil to paper do some serious thinking. Familiarize yourself with the area. Carefully consider its possibilities—and its limitations. No use trying to grow water lilies in shade or rhododendrons on outcrops of limestone. Consider also the purposes you wish your home grounds to serve. Ordinarily you will need a service area to accommodate a laundry yard, delivery entrance, and perhaps a separate garage or tool shed. This service area should be screened by shrubbery, hedge, or maybe a vine-covered trellis.

The front yard is usually somewhat public, largely visible from the street. It should contribute its part to the beauty and landscaped effect of the community. Nothing is better than a well-kept lawn as a main front feature. Appropriately placed shade trees, and discreetly located shrubbery may frame the house and lot. Boundary hedges are often advantageous. A foundation planting that weds the house to the ground completes the picture.

Let restraint be the keynote. Plant too little rather than too much. Above all do not spot single bushes, trees, or flower beds indiscriminately on the lawn. Such treatment produces a confused landscape.

Avoid using too many different types of plants in the foundation planting. Be particularly wary of highly colored evergreens such as golden arborvitaes, blue spruces, and the like. They do not blend well. Gazing globes, sundials, statues, and similar ornaments are out of place in the front yard.

The location of the driveway and of the path to the front door must be carefully considered. On a narrow lot place the driveway at one side and let the pathway branch from it near the house. A front lawn divided by a central path appears narrower than it really is.

The back garden is normally the private area—the part that you use for outdoor living. Screen it discreetly to assure reasonable privacy and to block undesirable views. A fairly spacious lawn near the house is most often desirable. This lawn should be defined in some way—by hedge, fence, or shrubbery. An open area that is not limited fails to provide a sense of enclosure, and a desirable, outdoor, living-room effect.

You will use the back lawn for sitting, sun bathing, and eating outdoors. A shade tree or two will be appreciated there. Flower borders may be located at its margins. A sundial, seat, statue, fountain, or pool can often be placed to provide a center of interest.

The back lawn should be an outdoor extension of the interior of the home approached via a porch or terrace, from the living room if possible. On larger lots the private part of the garden includes not only the outdoor living room, but areas that extend beyond it to the rear and to the side of the house. These may include a rose, rock, herb, cut-flower, vegetable, or other special garden as well as naturally landscaped areas.

The problem you face as a designer is to tie all parts of your home grounds into one satisfying, congruous whole, and to appropriately define its boundaries. Simplicity, livability, and ease of maintenance are points to bear in mind. Avoid the common error of setting out too many trees, shrubs, and evergreens in too small areas. A few, fairly sizable items may be very much more effective, not more expensive, and if well placed will not become spoiled by crowding as the years pass.

But first plan your new garden on paper. It is easier to correct mistakes there than on the ground. Graph paper ruled in small squares is useful for the purpose.

Renovating an Old Garden. If you are inexperienced and have to renovate an old garden, the task may seem to be more formidable than that of creating a new garden. But wait a minute. Maybe there is more to be salvaged than you think. In the old garden, overcrowded and long neglected though it may be, there are probably some well established trees and shrubs which, if given a reasonable chance, will become prized features. Among the tangle of weeds and overgrown shrubbery you may find perennials of various kinds that have persisted through the years of neglect, and need only reasonable care to induce them to bloom freely. Bulbs of daffodils, lilies, and other hardy kinds may be in the ground without, perhaps, their leaves showing at the time you view the garden. The lawn, possibly, is capable of responding to treatment less drastic than expensive remaking. An old, overgrown garden is a challenge. Meet it squarely. It can give you as much fun as making over an old house.

The first need of the garden renovator is patience. You cannot do it all at once. You must get to know what plants are in the garden before you discard any, and this may mean living with it through a season. Even the most experienced cannot distinguish choice lilacs from poorer kinds, better varieties of day lilies from semiwild ones, or worthwhile chrysanthemums from worthless ones by examining the foliage alone. To evaluate these and many other flowers, it is necessary to see them in bloom. And this probably involves waiting.

However, you need not be idle. There are surely some things that you can do right away in any neglected garden. The cleaning away of weeds, cutting out of unwanted material, and preliminary pruning, for instance. Cut out only those trees, shrubs, and vines that you are certain you do not want: straggly, bare-at-the-bottom evergreens of kinds that will not respond to pruning for instance, and specimens so badly placed that you must remove them, but which you cannot, or do not want, to transplant.

Preliminary pruning must also be done cautiously if you do not know the plants. Dead branches may be cut out. Trees and shrubs which are obviously overcrowded may be moderately thinned. But avoid any general "butchering." An urge for tidiness may result in irreparable harm to valuable specimens.

The really important thing is to get to know what kinds of plants you have. Some you may recognize. Others may be identified for you by experienced gardeners. In still other cases it may be necessary to send samples for identification to a botanical garden, or to your State Agricultural Experiment Station. Once you know what the plants in your garden are, you can proceed intelligently. Each can be treated according to its needs. When renovating a garden, consider basic design just as you do when making a new garden. If alteration is needed, try to retain or adapt the best features of the present layout.

Pruning based on a knowledge of the plants and their needs will require attention. In some cases you may prune severely. Straggly hedges of privet or barberry may be cut nearly to the ground, as well as old, gangling lilacs. Overgrown shrubs of many kinds may be severely thinned. Some other trees and shrubs are better if left unpruned. Read the chapter on pruning in this book before you tackle the job.

Look the old garden over for the presence of blights and pests, black spots on roses and scale insects on *Euonymus,* for example. Take suitable steps to bring these under control.

I have found it a good plan, when making over old gardens, to establish nursery areas. Into these I transplant plants temporarily or divisions of plants that cannot, at the time, be set in their permanent places. They grow into shapely specimens and a few months or a year later, when their permanent places are ready, they are available for replanting.

Garden Soils

✤✤

An adequate depth of fertile soil in good condition is the basis of practically all gardening. Without it the plants you grow will be less vigorous and less healthy than they should be. To maintain fertility, do your utmost to provide the best soil.

Nearly all soils can be improved tremendously by intelligent management. Treatments employed to do this include draining, loosening and turning, adding humus, fertilizing, and liming.

Draining. Roots need air as well as moisture. Plants that grow naturally in ponds and bogs obtain air from the water in which they grow. Most plants cannot do this. Their roots rot and die if they are immersed for long. That is why subsurface drainage of the soil is important.

If you suspect your soil is waterlogged or poorly drained, dig test holes (two feet square and two feet deep) here and there; build a ridge of soil around each to prevent surface water from draining in, and cover with a watertight cover. If free water stands in the holes closer than two feet to the surface for weeks together, artificial drainage is usually needed. Agricultural drain tiles are best for providing this. First, locate an outlet below the lowest point to be drained. This may be a pond, stream, ditch, sewer, or other feature that permits disposal of the surplus water. Working backwards from the outlet, dig a system of ditches with bottoms that slope gradually upwards at a rate of four to six inches for each hundred running feet. At the outlet the ditch may be two to three feet deep. It should not be less than eighteen inches below ground level at any point. Make the bottoms of the ditches firm; then lay the drain tiles. Butt their ends together but use no cement, because the water to be carried away must enter the drain through the joints. Cover the drain with cinders or gravel, then fill with regular soil. Space the drains from eighteen to thirty feet apart. In heavy clay soils, closer spacing is needed. Drains are usually laid in herringbone pattern. The main drain may be four to six inches in bore, the side or feeder drains, three to four inches.

Loosening and Turning. Loosening and turning the soil admits air, improves drainage, permits thorough mixing in of humus, brings fresh portions of the soil to the surface to be improved by weathering, and buries weeds. Normally, this should be done before planting.

Soils are classified as light, medium, and heavy, according to the relative ease with which they may be worked. Sandy soils which break apart and fall readily before tools are light. Clays which stick to tools and are hard to work are heavy. Medium soils (loams) come between these extremes, being light loams if sand clearly predominates, heavy if they resemble clay.

Heavy soils benefit greatly from weathering and particularly from frost. Whenever possible, turn them over in fall and leave their surface rough over winter. It is usually better not to spade light soils until shortly before planting.

Shallow soils, if not underlaid with solid rock, may be deepened by proper working. If your soil is shallow, avoid bringing up and mixing with the topsoil more than an inch or two of poor subsoil at any one time. This, however, you may do with advantage. In other words, if your topsoil is six inches deep and overlies an infertile subsoil, turn it to a depth of seven or eight inches and add plenty of humus material. In a year you will have seven or eight inches of topsoil. Then you may turn it over to a depth of nine or ten inches, again adding humus, thus again deepening the topsoil. And so on until you reach the maximum depth at which your implements will operate.

This gradual deepening works well in areas devoted to annual crops, but not where permanent crops are planted. In such places double-digging will improve the subsoil in place, at one time, and without mixing it with the topsoil.

How to Spade. Suppose you are going to spade a piece of ground. It is too small to plow or rototill. First drive a stake at each corner. Next stretch a line (or piece of strong string) from stake to stake. Mark along this by chopping a groove into the ground with the bottom edge of the spade. This defines the area. Dig a trench or ditch across one end of the plot and dump the excavated soil at the other end, just outside the marked-off area. Make the trench a foot wide and as deep as the blade of the spade is long. If the plot is weedy, skim off the weeds back from the edge of the trench eight or nine inches and throw them into the bottom of the trench. Do the same with weeds close to the ends of the trench. Spread a layer of manure, compost or other humus material in the trench and begin spading. Except in stony ground you can do better with a spade than you can with a spading fork. The latter is the better tool for stony ground.

Begin at one end of the trench. Drive the blade of the tool almost vertically into the ground six or seven inches back from the edge of the trench. Thrust the blade downwards with all your weight behind it; don't depend upon stamping or kicking. When the tool is driven in as deeply as possible, pull backwards on the handle, drop one hand down the shaft to act as a fulcrum and to provide the lift necessary. Throw the soil well forward, at the same time turning it upside down so the surface soil is underneath and soil from beneath is brought to the top. Repeat this along the edge of the trench until the end is reached. Skim the weeds off alongside the end of the trench, spread manure or compost in it, and proceed as before. Continue trench after trench until the end of the plot is reached. Fill last trench with soil from the first.

Double-digging is done in the same way as single-digging, except that the trench is two to two and a half feet wide and is as deep as the topsoil or the spade blade, whichever is greater. One other difference: in double-digging, a four- to six-inch layer of manure or compost is spaded into the bottom of each trench, then another layer is spread along the bottom of the trench before the topsoil from the next trench is turned on it. In single-digging the soil is loosened and turned to the depth of the blade or a spade; in double-digging, to about twice the depth.

Plows and Rotary Tillers. The plow is an agricultural rather than a garden implement. Only operators of much acreage ordinarily use plows. Rotary tillers, on the other hand, are primarily garden implements. Small models designed for gardens of modest size do first class work, taking a great deal of hard labor out of gardening. You can loosen your soil and mix humus or other needed materials with the rotary tiller to a depth of ten inches or so with little effort. It takes the place of both plow and harrow and prepares a splendid seed bed.

Adding Humus. Humus is decayed organic matter—dark material that makes topsoil deeper in color than subsoil. Unless they contain an adequate amount of humus, light soils dry out fast and are leached of their nutrients; clay soils become compacted, fail to admit air, and cake and crack under the rain and sun. Humus breaks down in the soil and supplies nourishment for both plants and micro-organisms. Because of this, its supply is constantly depleted and must be replaced. Maintenance of a suitable proportion of humus in the soil is a major problem.

Two methods of adding humus are employed: (1) using dead (and usually, partially decayed) material; (2) turning under a growing crop (green manuring). Animal manure, compost, leaf mold, peat moss, and natural humus obtained from bogs and lakes are the chief dead materials employed. Almost anything that has lived, died, and decayed can be used. Be sure to use enough. In areas given over to annual crops a two- or three-inch layer turned under each year is usually not excessive. Amounts in excess of this can often be used profitably when preparing for perennial crops. If manure or other humus material is added shortly before planting, see that it is pretty well decayed. Undecayed or semidecayed material should be used only if several weeks are to elapse before planting. Never place manure close to roots unless it is thoroughly decayed. When humus materials are not plentiful, green manures are good substitutes. Most important for gardens is winter rye, which is commonly sown in fall and turned under in early spring. Both the tops and the root systems decay and turn to humus which improves the soil immensely. Good, green manures for summer are buckwheat, oats, soybeans, and cow peas. Sow green manure crops whenever the ground is expected to be vacant for a few weeks. Turn them under while they are yet succulent, and before they become too woody or otherwise difficult to handle. Always spade green manures under two or three weeks before you plant.

Fertilizers. Materials added to the soil to provide humus also supply nutrient elements. This is especially true of animal manures. Often, however, they do not supply enough, and scarcely do they ever contain the required elements in needed proportions. Fertilizers are used to correct this, and to supplement nourishment that manures, composts, green manures, etc., add to the soil. Elements most often deficient are nitrogen, phosphorus, and potassium. Fertilizers that contain all of these are known as complete fertilizers. On fertilizer containers you will find a formula consisting of three numbers. The first states the percentage of nitrogen; the second, the percentage of available phosphoric acid; the third, the percentage of water soluble potash. Fertilizers such as those numbered

5-10-5 or 4-12-4 are good, general purpose fertilizers. For special purposes other formulas are used. For some areas in North America special fertilizers containing trace elements deficient in the native soil, such as boron, are prepared. These are available locally. There are also fertilizers, useful for particular purposes, that contain only one or two of the three important elements. While the formula indicates the proportions in which nitrogen, phosphorus, and potassium occur, it does not show the speed with which they become available to the plant. This is particularly important with nitrogen. If the nitrogen content of a fertilizer is quickly available, its effect is immediate but not long-lasting; if it occurs in the form of an organic material, it is much slower acting but continues to stimulate the plant over a much longer period. Most complete, commercial fertilizers contain quickly available nitrogen as well as more slowly available nitrogen. Such fertilizers are generally best for the garden. Fertilizers are not substitutes for humus nor can manure and other organic material completely or economically do the work of fertilizers. You will need both.

Liming. Do not use lime unless a soil test indicates it is needed. Have such tests made yearly for pH (acidity or alkalinity).

Lime neutralizes acidity. Most (but not all) plants get along well in a soil that is approximately neutral. Some must have distinctly acid soil. Lime is not only of benefit in correcting acidity, but also greatly improves the physical condition of heavy soils, helps release certain plant foods found in unusable compounds, and provides calcium. Use hydrated lime on heavy soils, and ground limestone on light soils, but only in quantities that tests show are desirable. Use gypsum where the beneficial effects of lime are needed, but it is not desirable to make the soil more alkaline.

Planting a Tree

Shade trees such as oaks, elms, and maples, and flowering trees such as magnolias, crabs, and dogwoods need care. It is not enough to let them just look after themselves.

If well located they add to the beauty and cash value of your property. Therefore, it pays to give them the attention they need. Cultivate your trees. Don't let them take pot luck.

Before planting new trees consider carefully which are best suited for your purpose. Obtain some idea of their ultimate height and shape. Are they fast-growing or slow-growing? Is their wood brittle and subject to storm damage? Are their roots likely to clog drains? Are they susceptible to diseases or insects?

Get to know also if they are adapted to your soil and location, and if they are easy or difficult to transplant.

You may not be able to get a tree that has every good quality but if you set up a balance sheet of comparative virtues you can choose one that rates highly.

Let price be a secondary consideration. A good tree lasts a long time. If you cannot afford the kind you want in the size you would like take a smaller specimen rather than a poor substitute. You will be amazed how quickly it will grow if you look after it. And it's fun watching the development of a tree you have planted yourself.

Don't skimp on preparing the hole for a new tree. Dig it wide enough to accommodate the roots when fully spread out with at least a foot extra all around, and more if it is a big specimen or if the soil is poor. Break the bottom of the hole with a spading fork and mix plenty of rotted manure or compost with the undersoil. Prepare the hole in advance of planting.

Make sure the tree is dug with an ample mass of healthy roots. The more roots that can be saved the better. The fine, fibrous, feeding roots are especially important. With most deciduous (non-evergreen) trees of ordinary planting size it is not necessary to move a ball of earth. The roots are shaken or combed free of soil. Protect the bare roots from drying by wrapping them in moist burlap, wet hay, or similar material. If you cannot plant such trees right away, heel them in (set them closely together and cover the roots with soil). Specimens of deciduous trees larger than ordinary planting size are usually dug with a large ball of earth. Then the outer portion is combed with a fork so that a comparatively small, center ball remains with bare roots protruding all around. Wrap these roots to keep them moist.

At planting time cut off cleanly any broken root ends. Reduce the top somewhat by removing unwanted branches and by shortening side branches a bit. In some cases the leader or central growing shoot may be shortened slightly also.

Set the tree at the same depth or perhaps an inch deeper than it was in the nursery. Work good topsoil enriched with humus and perhaps a little bone meal among its roots but do not use fertilizer. Pack the soil firmly. Do not complete the surface leveling at once. Leave a slight depression where the hole was, and fill this with water two or three times to settle the soil about the roots.

Staking or guying with three wires (threaded through old rubber hose where they go around the trunk) may be needed to make the newly planted tree secure. To complete the job, mulch the soil with a layer of compost, old manure or peat moss.

The best time to plant is during leaf drop in fall, or in spring two or three weeks before the buds burst. Choose cloudy weather, if possible. Sun and wind dry the roots.

GOOD SHADE TREES

CHINESE ELM (*Ulmus pumila*). Moderate size. Fast grower. Good city tree.

CRIMSON KING MAPLE (*Acer platanoides Crimson King*). Fine variety of Norwegian maple. Deep, purple-red foliage. Thrives in ordinary soil. Like all maples, roots at surface; hence difficult to grow anything under when big.

HONEY LOCUST (*Gleditsia triacanthos*). Large, of same form as American elm and best substitute for it. Flowers fragrant. A thornless as well as normally thorny type is available. Good city tree.

JAPANESE PAGODA TREE (*Sophora japonica*). Large, roundheaded, branches spreading. Showy white flowers in summer. Stands heat and drought well.

PIN OAK (*Quercus palustris*). Large but comparatively narrow. Grows fairly fast. Will thrive in moist soil. Good city tree.

RED MAPLE (*Acer rubrum*). Large. Difficult to grow anything under. Attractive in bloom and in fall color. Thrives in moist or wet soils.

RED OAK (*Quercus borealis*). Large, roundheaded. Grows fairly fast. Good fall color.

SASSAFRAS (*Sassafras albidum*). Tall but quite slender. Good fall color. Difficult to transplant. Set out young trees only. Prefers light soils.

SMALL-LEAVED LINDEN (*Tilia cordata*). Large, but stands pruning well. Will not thrive in dry soil. Flowers fragrant. Good city tree.

GOOD SMALL FLOWERING TREES

ENGLISH HAWTHORN (*Crataegus oxyacantha Pauls Scarlet*). Pink flowers in spring.

FLOWERING CRABS (*Malus*). White or pink flowers in spring. Many excellent varieties. Attractive in fruit. Good kinds are *spectabilis, hupehensis, niedzwetsck-yana* and *scheideckeri.*

FLOWERING DOGWOOD (*Cornus florida*). White or pink flowers in spring. Red berries and good foliage color in fall. Needs fairly moist good soil. Transplant with ball of earth.

JAPANESE CHERRIES (*Prunus*). White or pink flowers in spring. Many excellent varieties. Good kinds are *Kwanzan, Fugenzo* and *Shirofugen.* Difficult to transplant except when small.

JAPANESE FLOWERING DOGWOOD (*Cornus kousa*). White flowers. Blooms one month later than native flowering dogwood. Less stiff in habit. Attractive raspberry-like fruit.

MAGNOLIA (*Magnolia soulangeana*). Large pink or purple-pink flowers in spring. Transplant in spring only.

SILVER BELL (*Halesia monticola*). White flowers in spring. Likes good soil.

WASHINGTON THORN (*Crataegus phaenopyrum*). White flowers in spring. Long-lasting red fruits in fall.

WITCH-HAZEL, CHINESE (*Hamamelis mollis*). Yellow flowers in late winter.

WITCH-HAZEL, JAPANESE (*Hamamelis japonica*). Yellow flowers in late winter.

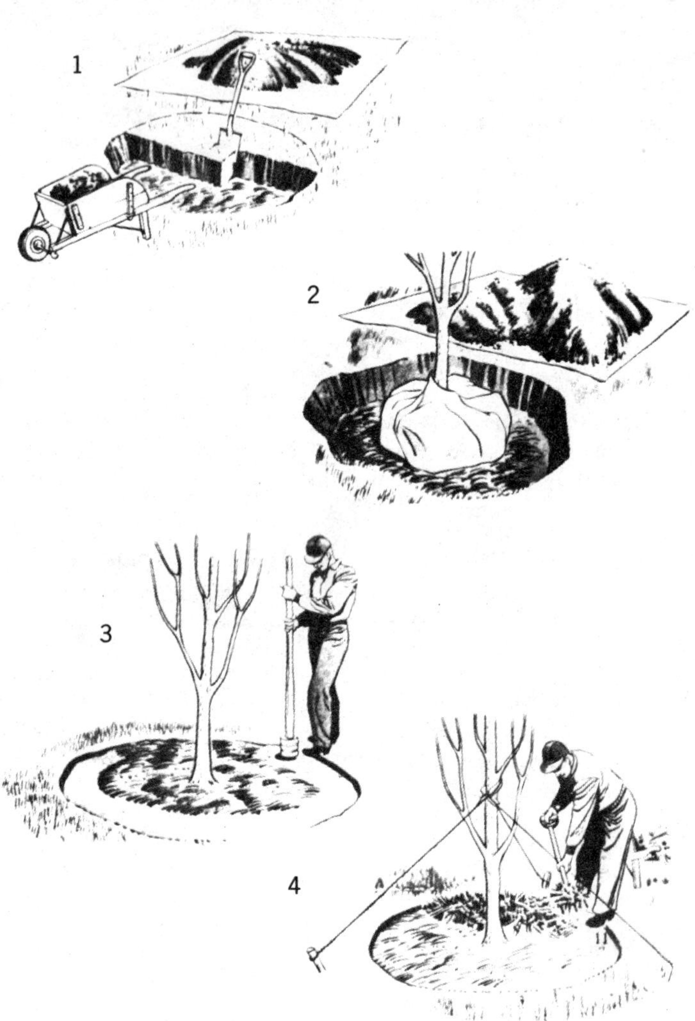

1. To plant a tree, first dig a hole deep enough for tne roots. Spade bottom of hole, mix in plenty of manure and humus. 2. Place tree in hole. Loosen burlap. Leave bottom sacking to rot. 3. With roots spread in natural growth position, fill hole with topsoil mixed with compost, humus or peat moss. Tamp fill. 4. Water thoroughly, let drain two hours, add more soil, top with mulch. Use guy wires to hold tree firmly in an upright position.

Shrubs for the Home Garden

Shrubs that drop their leaves each fall are deciduous. In every garden there is a place for some deciduous shrubs. You may use them in borders, beds, and as informal screens. Most of them flower attractively and many of them fruit profusely. They change with the seasons more than evergreens do. They provide lightness and grace. Many, such as lilacs and mock oranges, are good cut flowers.

Select your shrubs with care. Find out before planting how large each will eventually become, and allow space for its development.

Nondescript, ragged-looking shrubberies result from choosing poor kinds, and setting the plants too closely together.

Most shrubs grow remarkably fast if given a reasonable chance. Because of this it is usually best to plant young, vigorous specimens. Only in the case of such slow-growing kinds as azaleas does it pay to buy bigger plants to start. Not that large shrubs cannot be moved safely. Most of them can. But the labor involved adds to the cost, and is usually unwarranted.

Prepare the ground well. Spade the entire area if a bed or border is to be planted. Dig a large-sized hole for a

SHRUBS FOR THE GARDEN

Type of Shrubs	For Very Dry Soils	For Moist or Wet Soils	For Ordinary Soils	Approximate Height in Feet	Flower Color	Blooming Season	Good Fall Foliage Color	Attractive in Fruit	Needs Full Sun	Good for Shade	Withstands Light Shade	Kills Back But Renews Self Each Year in Cold Climates
Glossy Abelia (*Abelia grandiflora*)			✓	3 to 6	blush (fragrant)	summer & fall	✓	✓			✓	✓
False Indigo (*Amorpha fruticosa*)	✓			12	purple	late spring			✓			
Red Chokeberry (*Aronia arbutifolia*)		✓		10	white	spring		✓			✓	
*Korean Azalea (*Azalea mucronulata*)			✓	6	rosy lavender	early spring					✓	
*Flame azalea (*Azalea calendulacea*)			✓	10	orange to scarlet	spring					✓	
*Pinxter-Flower (*Azalea nudiflora*)			✓	6	blush to pink (fragrant)	spring					✓	
*Royal Azalea (*Azalea schlippenbachii*)			✓	6 to 7	pink (fragrant)	spring					✓	
*Pinkshell Azalea (*Azalea vaseyi*)		✓		6	pink	early spring	✓				✓	
*Torch Azalea (*Azalea kaempferi*)			✓	6	orange-salmon	spring					✓	
*Swamp Honeysuckle (*Azalea viscosa*)		✓		8	pink or blush (fragrant)	early summer	✓				✓	
Japanese Barberry (*Berberis thunbergii*)			✓	6	yellow	spring	✓	✓			✓	
Fountain Buddleia (*Buddleia alternifolia*)			✓	15	lavender (fragrant)	early summer			✓			

*Require acid soil.

Butterfly Bush (*Buddleia davidi*)			√	15	white, pink, red & purple (fragrant)	summer & fall			√			√
Beauty-berry (*Callicarpa dichotoma* and *Callicarpa japonica*)			√	4 to 5				√	√			√
Bluebeard or Blue Spirea (*Caryopteris incana*)			√	4	blue	fall			√			√
Dwarf Flowering Quince (*Chaenomeles japonica*)			√	3	pink & red	spring		√	√			
Japanese Quince (*Chaenomeles lagenaria*)			√	8	pink, red & white	spring		√	√			
Sweet Pepperbush (*Clethra alnifolia*)		√		10	white (fragrant)	summer	√				√	
Tatarian Dogwood (*Cornus alba sibirica*)		√		8					√			
Golden Twig Dogwood (*Cornus stolonifera flaviramea*)		√		10					√			
Winter Hazel (*Corylopsis pauciflora*)			√ √	6	yellow (fragrant)	early spring	√		√			
Cotoneaster (*Cotoneaster hupehensis*)			√	6	white	spring	√	√	√			
(*Cotoneaster racemiflora*)			√	6	white	spring	√	√	√			
(*Cotoneaster horizontalis*)			√	8	white	spring		√	√			
(*Cotoneaster salicifolia floccosa*)			√	3	pink	spring	√	√	√			
			√	10	white	spring	√	√	√			
Broom (*Cytissus nigricans*)	√			4	yellow (fragrant)	summer			√			
Scotch Broom (*Cytissus scoparius*)	√			8	yellow (fragrant)	summer			√			
Deutzia (*Deutzia gracilis*)			√	4	white	late spring			√			
(*Deutzia lemoinei*)			√	6	white	late spring			√			
Enkianthus (*Enkianthus campanulatus*)		√		15	yellowish brown	spring	√				√	
(*Enkianthus perulatus*)		√		6	white	spring	√				√	

Type of Shrubs	For Very Dry Soils	For Moist or Wet Soils	For Ordinary Soils	Approximate Height in Feet	Flower Color	Blooming Season	Good Fall Foliage Color	Attractive in Fruit	Needs Full Sun	Good for Shade	Withstands Light Shade	Kills Back But Renews Self Each Year in Cold Climates
Corkbark Evonymus												
(Evonymus alatus)			✓	8			✓		✓			
(Evonymus alatus compactus)			✓	5			✓		✓			
Forsythia												
(Forsythia intermedia spectabilis)			✓	10	yellow	early spring			✓			
(Forsythia ovata)			✓	8	yellow	early spring			✓			
(Forsythia suspensa)			✓	10	yellow	early spring			✓			
Honeysuckle												
(Lonicera morrowii)			✓	6	white	spring		✓			✓	
(Lonicera standishii)			✓	6	white (fragrant)	early spring					✓	
(Lonicera tatarica)			✓	10	white or pink	spring		✓			✓	
Snowberry *(Symphoricarpos albus)*			✓	5	white	summer		✓		✓		
Starry Magnolia *(Magnolia stellata)*			✓	15	white	spring			✓			
Neillia *(Neillia sinensis)*			✓	5	white or	spring					✓	
Flowering Crab *(Malus sargentii)*			✓	6	white	spring		✓	✓			
Snow Wreath *(Neviusia alabamensis)*			✓	5	white	late spring					✓	
Mock Orange												
(Philadelphus coronarius)			✓	10	white (fragrant)	late spring					✓	
(Philadelphus virginalis)			✓	6	white (fragrant)	late spring					✓	
Beach Plum *(Prunus maritima)*	✓			10	white	spring		✓	✓			

Flowering Plum ***(Prunus triloba)***			✓	6	pink	spring			✓			
Jetbead ***(Rhodotypos tetrapetala)***			✓	6	white	late spring		✓			✓	
Shrub Roses ***(Rosa rugosa)***	✓			6	pink, red & white (fragrant)	late spring		✓	✓			
(Rosa spinosissima altaica)	✓			6	white (fragrant)	late spring		✓	✓			
Spiraea *(Spiraea prunifolia plena)*			✓	6	white	spring			✓			
(Spiraea vanhouttei)			✓	6	white	spring			✓			
(Spiraea Anthony Waterer)			✓	2½	pink	summer & fall			✓			
Sweetleaf ***(Symplocos paniculata)***			✓	20	white (fragrant)	spring		✓			✓	
Fothergilla ***(Fothergilla gardeni)***		✓		3	cream (fragrant)	spring (fragrant)	✓				✓	
(Fothergilla monticola)		✓		6	cream (fragrant)	spring (fragrant)	✓				✓	
Rose of Sharon ***(Hibiscus syriacus)***			✓	12	white, pink, lavender, blue & red	summer & fall			✓			
Hydrangea ***(Hydrangea paniculata)***			✓	15	white	summer & fall					✓	
†(Hydrangea macrophylla)			✓	8	white, blue & pink	summer & fall			✓			
(Hydrangea arborescens grandiflora)			✓	10	white	summer			✓			
St. Johns Wort ***(Hypericum frondosum)***			✓	4	yellow	summer & fall					✓	
Winterberry ***(Ilex verticillata)***		✓		10				✓				

†Do not thrive in dry soils.

Type of Shrubs	For Very Dry Soils	For Moist or Wet Soils	For Ordinary Soils	Approximate Height in Feet	Flower Color	Blooming Season	Good Fall Foliage Color	Attractive in Fruit	Needs Full Sun	Good for Shade	Withstands Light Shade	Kills Back But Renews Self Each Year in Cold Climates
Sweet-spire *(Itea virginica)*		✓		8	white (fragrant)	summer	✓		✓			
Jasmine *(Jasminum nudiflorum)*			✓	8	yellow	early spring			✓			
Kerria *(Kerria japonica)*			✓	6	yellow	late spring	✓				✓	
Beauty Bush *(Kolkwitzia amabilis)*			✓	8	pink	summer			✓			
Spice Bush *(Lindera benzoin)*		✓		12	yellow	early spring	✓			✓		
French Lilacs *(Syringa vulgaris)*			✓	20	white, lilac & purple (fragrant)	spring			✓			
Persian Lilac *(Syringa persica)*			✓	8	pink & lavender (fragrant)	spring			✓			
Tamarisks *(Tamarix parviflora)*	✓			15	pink	spring			✓			
(Tamarix odessiana)	✓			6	pink	late spring			✓			
(Tamarix pentandra)	✓			15	pink	summer			✓			
Viburnums *(Viburnum carlesii)*			✓	10	white (fragrant)	spring			✓			
(Viburnum tomentosum)			✓	10	white	late spring		✓			✓	
(Viburnum dilatatum)			✓	7	white	late spring		✓	✓			
Weigelia *(Weigelia florida hybrids)*			✓	8	pink	spring			✓			

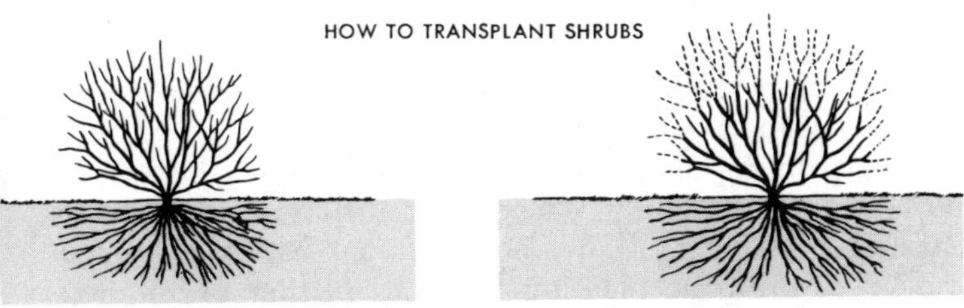

Shrub, left, is to be transplanted. First step is to prune away one third of the top, as shown at right.

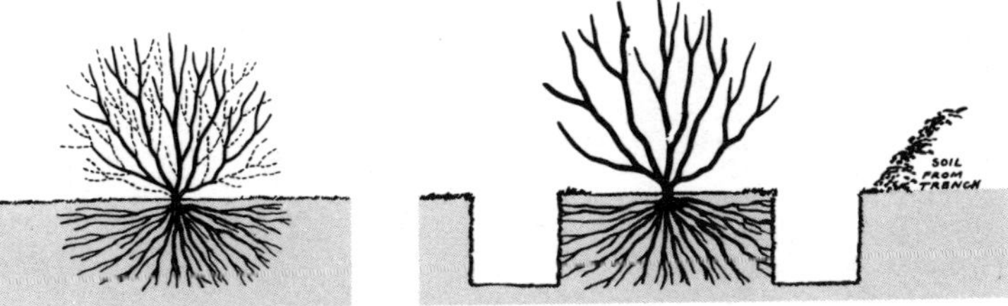

Or you may thin out one third of the branches *(left)*. Then dig a trench around the natural spread of the branches.

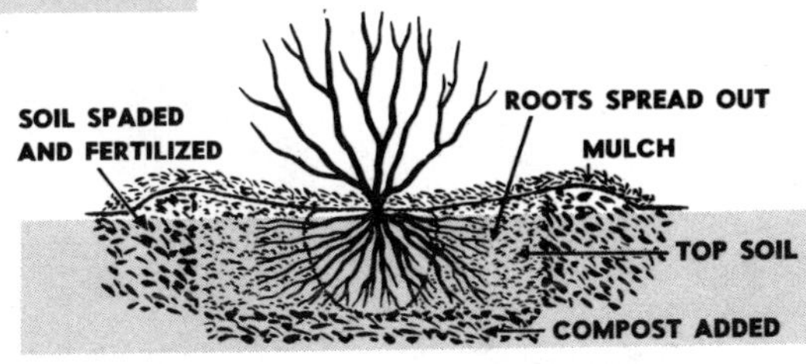

Comb most of the soil from the outer root mass *(left)*, then replant shrub as shown in diagram at right.

single specimen. Better a five-dollar-sized plant in a ten-dollar hole than vice versa.

The planting directions given for trees apply here also. Follow them carefully, except that shrubs rarely require staking or guying. Many, however, are better if pruned rather severely at planting time. Reduction of the top growth compensates for the loss of roots inevitable in transplanting. The best times to transplant shrubs are early fall and early spring.

Every Garden Should Have Evergreens

There is a solidity and feeling of permanence about evergreens that is not quite supplied by deciduous trees and shrubs. They seem to provide security and stability in the garden scheme of things.

As backgrounds to show off flowering plants to good advantage evergreens are superb. Many are unsurpassed as subjects for use in foundation plantings. Single specimens of pines, spruces, hollies, boxwood and many others can be breathtakingly magnificent. We use evergreens as hedges, groundcovers, and screens both to give privacy and to close out undesirable views. The "friendly evergreens," as one writer has dubbed them, are needed in every garden, so let's get to know something about them and how to use them.

Evergreens are divided into two great groups—the broad-leaved and the narrow-leaved. These designations are roughly descriptive but not entirely so. A few broad-leaved evergreens (such as heather) actually have foliage that is narrower than the leaves of some narrow-leaved evergreens, for example the plum-yew (*Cephalotaxus*). But these are exceptions.

True narrow-leaved evergreens are all conifers (using the term in its broad sense). They do not have what are usually considered to be flowers. Here belong the pines, spruces, firs, yews, junipers and arborvitaes.

Broad-leaved evergreens normally bear flowers and these are often very beautiful, as for example those of rhododendrons, mountain laurel, and camellias. Where winters are severe, the number of broad-leaved evergreens that can be grown is strictly limited. In more favored climates the garden maker has a much wider choice.

Evergreens for hedges and groundcovers are discussed elsewhere in this book. Here we shall consider their other uses and one of the chief of these is in foundation plantings.

Choose the kinds you use for this purpose with great care. Where permanently low plants are wanted don't set out young specimens of tall growing kinds. If you do, they will become so overgrown in a few years that they will have to be removed and replaced. It's wiser and less expensive to plant suitable varieties in the beginning: kinds that will remain low, or at least that can be kept low by proper pruning. And remember, not all evergreens can be pruned without harming them and detracting from their beauty.

In arranging your foundation planting avoid using too many different kinds of plants. To do so gives a "spotty" effect. And above all, do not splurge on highly colored types. Golden arborvitaes and silver cypresses that look cute in the nursery surrounded by lots of their kind or by oceans of green can be mighty hard to live with near your own front door. They shout too loud. They don't give their neighbors a chance.

Evergreens in a foundation planting should blend, and form comfortable billowy masses with taller accents only where needed as, for example, at the corners of the house.

If the house reaches high from the ground, tall corner accents are usually advantageous, but long low houses are improved by sticking to plants of more horizontal habit. The evergreens in your foundation planting must not only blend, but also provide a suitable background for whatever flowering plants you use—azaleas, tulips, or perhaps

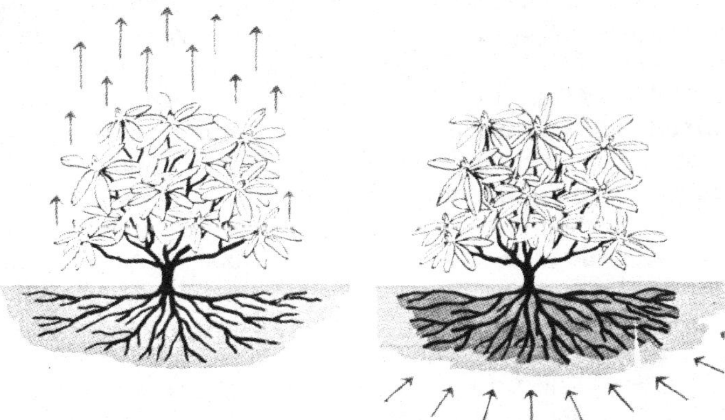

Evergreens give off water vapor through their leaves. In summer this loss is made good by water absorbed through roots. But in winter the frozen ground yields less water.

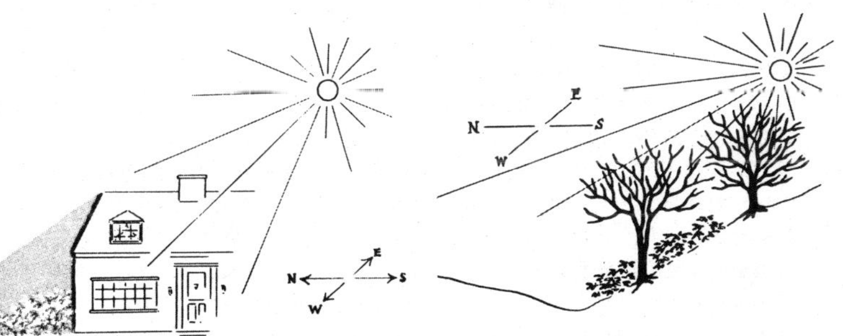

That's why evergreen leaves "burn" in winter—through loss of too much water. Prevent this by planting in shade or under trees on north or west slopes.

geraniums. Think of that when you plan your planting.

One more point. Don't overplant. Leave room for the newly set evergreens to grow. At a later date, if they do begin to crowd, transplant some of them or chop out a few if need be. Few plants are spoiled as quickly as evergreens that are crowded. The trick is to do something about it before they are harmed, before they have lost their foliage on one or more sides.

As informal screens and windbreaks, evergreens possess the supreme advantage of remaining good the year round. Such plantings are often preferable to strictly sheared hedges because they divide the landscape less sharply.

For screening, choose kinds that retain their lower branches. Select such plants also with an eye to their ultimate height and to the type of soil and location they prefer. Pines, junipers, and some others simply must have plenty of light and air. Hemlocks and rhododendrons typify kinds that need, or at least will stand, shade. It's no use planting acid soil plants in alkaline regions or lovers of moisture in dry, thirsty soils.

And in making screen plantings bear in mind that plants grow and need more room. To obtain a reasonably quick screen you may set out large plants to begin with and space them fairly wide apart; or set out smaller specimens closer together than is good for them, then thin them out later. The latter sounds attractive but the labor involved in transplanting plus a very natural disinclination to disturb an arrangement that still looks good often prevents it from being done. Too often plantings made with the intention of thinning them out later are left to deteriorate for lack of timely attention.

But it is not only as screens and background that evergreens may be grouped. The smaller kinds are also lovely in beds and borders in the fore- and middle-foreground. Flowering evergreens such as heathers and *Daphne cneorum* are especially effective when so used.

Specimen evergreens, well located and free standing, add immensely to the garden picture. Under these circumstances their beauty, grace, and dignity is emphasized.

They are not just part of a "planting." They are individuals. Such specimens need careful placing so they will have room to develop symmetrically.

When full grown they should be in scale with the property and with the garden picture. Don't plant a couple of Norway spruces which later may have a spread of fifty feet on a front plot measuring fifty by twenty-five feet. Select something smaller.

Planting. Planting evergreens differs from planting non-evergreens in one important particular. Except in the tiniest seedling sizes, they should never be handled bare-rooted. They should always have a good ball of earth attached to their roots. And this ball should not be broken or disturbed. Do not comb the roots around the outside of the ball free of soil as is recommended for deciduous trees and shrubs. Keep the ball intact.

To ensure this see that the ball is wrapped tightly in burlap and handle the plant carefully so there is no danger of the soil cracking across or loosening or breaking apart.

Never pick up an evergreen, or indeed any other balled plant, by its top or trunk. Always take hold of the ball itself when the plant has to be lifted or moved.

If evergreens cannot be planted immediately after they are dug stand them closely together in a shady place, away from sweeping winds, and pack the balls around with moist leaves, straw, hay or similar material. Sprinkle the tops with water two or three times a day.

It is not usual to cut back evergreens at planting time and with many kinds it is not practicable. But some evergreens can be so treated and it is advantageous if they must be moved with a comparatively small root ball to cut them back. This may also be done if they are straggly, unshapely specimens.

Dig the holes quite large. Allow a foot or more of space around the outside of the ball for packing in new soil. Break up the bottom of the hole and add plenty of humus material. Set the plant so that when planted it will not be more than an inch deeper than it was before. Unwrap the burlap and cut it away so that the piece immediately beneath the ball remains undisturbed. It will rot in the soil. Pack firmly around the ball some good top soil mixed with about one-third part humus, compost, peat moss, or very rotted manure. Do not use fresh manure.

When the hole is three-quarters filled with soil, fill it with water three or four times and allow it to drain for an hour or two before completing the job. Then fill in more soil and finish off the surface so there is a slight depression around the trunk and a rim around the outside of the hole-that-was. This facilitates future waterings.

Always mulch evergreens after planting. A two or three inch layer of leaf mold, compost, peat moss or other suitable material keeps the soil evenly moist and encourages favorable root action.

The most favorable times to transplant evergreens are in spring just before new growth begins or in late summer or early fall after the season's new growth has matured and become firm.

It is especially important that newly-planted evergreens never suffer for lack of moisture during the first year after planting.

Caring for Evergreens. All evergreens benefit if the soil around them is kept mulched. Digging or otherwise disturbing the roots of evergreens is very harmful. If the late summer and fall is dry see that evergreens are well watered. Watch out for lace-bug on rhododendrons, red spider on spruces, junipers and hemlocks and for first signs of other pests and diseases and take prompt remedial measures if they appear. It's no use spraying unless the plants are threatened.

Narrow-Leaved Evergreens

FIRS. Need rich, moist soil and unpolluted atmosphere. Not good for city conditions. Splendid as single specimens. Attain heights of 75 feet and more. Among the best are White Fir; Nordmann Fir, and Nikko Fir.

DOUGLAS FIR. Thrives in ordinary soil. An attractive fast-growing evergreen tree. Withstands city conditions fairly well. Not a true fir.

SPRUCES. Require good soil, neither wet nor excessively dry. Most form sizable trees but also many dwarf varieties. Among the best are Engelmann Spruce, Oriental Spruce and White Spruce. For windbreaks, Norway Spruce. Colorado Blue Spruce is popular.

PINES. Mostly adapted for dryish soils and exposed situations. Stand city conditions fairly well. Among the best are White Pine, Swiss Stone Pine, Austrian Pine, Red Pine and Scotch Pine. Mugho Pine is a good dwarf. Japanese Black Pine is excellent for seashore.

JUNIPERS. Need good drainage and thrive in rather poor, dry soils. They need full sun. Many kinds are available in a wide assortment of forms, shapes and colorings. Among the best are Chinese Juniper, Pfitzer Juniper, Sargent Juniper, Meyer Juniper and Eastern Red-cedar.

CYPRESSES (*Including Biotas and Retinisporas*). Need protection from sweeping wind. They stand some shade. Among the best are Sawara Cypress, Hinoki Cypress, Dwarf Hinoki Cypress, Nootka Cypress and, for mild climates, Lawson Cypress.

CEDARS. Need warm, rich soils. Magnificent as specimens. Tenderest is the Deodar. A hardy form of the Cedar of Lebanon thrives in Massachusetts. The Atlantic Cedar is intermediate in hardiness.

HEMLOCKS. Need fairly moist, well-drained soils, protection from sweeping winds. Stand shade better than most narrow-leaved evergreens. All are excellent. Sargents Weeping Hemlock is low and attractive.

ARBORVITAES. Need moist soil. American arborvitae is hardiest of evergreens. Many varieties available. Most discolor in winter.

YEWS. Thrive in ordinary soils. Stand sun or shade. Withstand city conditions well. Numerous varieties available. Most important are Upright Japanese Yew, Spreading Japanese Yew, Dwarf Japanese Yew, Hick's Yew, and Spreading English Yew. The Upright English Yew and the Irish Yew are less hardy.

A SELECTION OF BROAD-LEAVED EVERGREENS

Name of Shrub	For Full Sun	Prefers Light Shade	For Sun or Shade	Needs or Prefers Acid Soil	Needs Fairly Moist Soil	Needs Well-Drained Soil, Not Too Dry	Has Attractive Fruits	Color of Flowers	Blooming Season	Hardy North	Needs Sheltered Position or Protection North	Suitable for Mild Climates Only	Height in Feet
Wintergreen Barberry (*Berberis julianae*)			✓			✓		yellow	spring		✓		6
Warty Barberry (*Berberis verruculosa*)			✓			✓		yellow	spring		✓		3
Japanese Boxwood (*Buxus microphylla japonica*)			✓			✓					✓		15
Common Boxwood (*Buxus sempervirens*)			✓			✓					✓		18
Camellia (*Camellia japonica*)		✓		✓	✓			white, pink and red	spring			✓	20
(*Camellia sasanqua*)		✓		✓	✓			white, pink and red	winter			✓	15
Mexican-orange (*choisya ternata*)	✓					✓		white (fragrant)	summer			✓	10
Rock-rose (*Cistus ladaniferus maculatus*)	✓					✓		white and red	summer		✓		5
(*Cistus laurifolius*)	✓					✓		white	summer			✓	8
Japanese Oleaster (*Elaeagnus pungens*)			✓			✓	✓	cream (fragrant)	summer			✓	10

Name of Shrub	For Full Sun	Prefers Light Shade	For Sun or Shade	Needs or Prefers Acid Soil	Needs Fairly Moist Soil	Needs Well-Drained Soil, Not Too Dry	Has Attractive Fruits	Color of Flowers	Blooming Season	Hardy North	Needs Sheltered Position or Protection North	Suitable for Mild Climates Only	Height in Feet
Cape Jasmine (*Gardenia florida*)			✓	✓		✓		white (fragrant)	summer			✓	6
*English Holly (*Ilex aquifolium*)			✓			✓	✓				✓		30
*Dahoon (*Ilex cassine*)			✓			✓	✓					✓	25
*Chinese Holly (*Ilex cornuta*)			✓			✓	✓				✓		12
Japanese Holly (*Ilex crenata*)			✓			✓					✓		20
Inkberry (*Ilex glabra*)			✓		✓					✓			6
*American Holly (*Ilex opaca*)			✓			✓	✓				✓		40
Mountain Laurel (*Kalmia latifolia*)		✓		✓		✓		pink	late spring	✓			20
Drooping Leucothoe (*Leucothoe catesbaei*)		✓		✓	✓			white	spring	✓			5
Japanese Privet (*Ligustrum japonicum*)			✓			✓	✓	white	summer			✓	12
Bull Bay *Magnolia grandiflora*)			✓			✓		white	summer			✓	80
Oregon Grape-holly (*Mahonia aquifolium*)		✓				✓	✓	yellow	spring		✓		4

*It is usually necessary to have male and female plants of hollies growing near together to ensure fruiting.

Name of Shrub	For Full Sun	Prefers Light Shade	For Sun or Shade	Needs or Prefers Acid Soil	Needs Fairly Moist Soil	Needs Well-Drained Soil, Not Too Dry	Has Attractive Fruits	Color of Flowers	Blooming Season	Hardy North	Needs Sheltered Position or Protection North	Suitable for Mild Climates Only	Height in Feet
Nandina (*Nandina domestica*)			✓		✓		✓	white	early summer			✓	6
Osmanthus (*Osmanthus ilicifolius*)			✓			✓		white (fragrant)	summer			✓	20
Mountain Andromeda (*Pieris floribunda*)		✓		✓	✓			white	spring	✓			5
Japanese Andromeda (*Pieris japonica*)		✓		✓	✓			white	spring		✓		10
Laland Firethorn (*Pyracantha coccinea lalandi*)			✓			✓	✓	white	spring		✓		8
Japanese Pittosporum (*Pittosporum tobira*)			✓			✓		cream (fragrant)	spring			✓	10
Cherry Laurel (*Prunus laurocerasus*)			✓			✓		white (fragrant)	summer			✓	20
India Hawthorn (*Raphiolepis indica*)			✓			✓		pink	spring			✓	5
Carolina Rhododendron (*Rhododendron caroliniana*)		✓		✓	✓			pink	spring	✓			6
Catawba Rhododendron (*Rhododendron catawbiense*) and its hybrids.		✓		✓	✓			white, pink, and red	late spring	✓			8
Rosebay Rhododendron (*Rhododendron maximum*)		✓		✓	✓			white or pink	early summer	✓			25
Indian Azaleas (*Rhododendron indicum*)		✓		✓	✓			white, pink, red	spring			✓	6

*It is usually necessary to have male and female plants of hollies growing near together to ensure fruiting.

Your Lawn—How to Make and Care for It

A good lawn sets off a garden to its best advantage. Like a carpet in a well-furnished room it provides a "finish" to the picture, a delightful feeling of homeyness. Outdoor carpets of grass, like indoor ones of other kinds, cost money to install and maintain. They are worth it.

The basis of any good permanent turf is thorough preparation. Without that its maintenance can be a heartbreaking job indeed. You probably know gardeners who struggle with their lawns year after year—sprinkling fertilizer, spreading lime, sowing seeds hopefully each spring. They try to do all the books say, so far as providing maintenance goes, but never attain more than a mangy apology for a real lawn.

If you are one of these gardeners, take heart. You can have a good lawn if you will do a real job of making it in the first place. Thorough preparation cuts down immensely on future maintenance.

Provide a good depth of rich soil. Establish healthy, luxuriant turf, and crab grass cannot compete with your fine lawn.

Turf experts may tell you a good lawn can be maintained on as little as four inches of rich topsoil. And so it can. But to do this needs meticulous attention throughout each season in fertilizing and watering.

If possible see that the topsoil is reasonably good to a depth of at least eight and preferably ten inches.

Making a New Lawn. Now let's take up the question of making a new lawn from scratch. Perhaps you have built a new house. The builders have left. The site may or may not be roughly graded. Almost certainly the ground has been churned and compacted by trucks, excavating machinery, bulldozers and other heavy equipment. It is in no physical condition to support the growth of grass.

Your greatest enemy is impatience. You want a nice lawn and right away. Pause a while. There is no way of restoring immediately the physical condition of soil that has been mauled by heavy machinery, particularly if it is a clayish soil. It takes time.

Something can be done. You can loosen it, and mix in humus and fertilizer. That helps, but it won't take the place of time.

My advice to those making lawns on soil that has been much compacted is to delay several months before sowing the permanent grass seed. Meantime, sow one or two crops of rye grass or other green manure crop, and turn these under. Prepare the soil for the green manure just as you would for sowing a lawn where the soil has not been compacted.

When making a new lawn, make sure the sub-surface drainage is good. A wet lawn will be a mossy lawn with a poor growth of grass. Wet ground needs land drains.

Secondly, decide what the finished grades are to be. If possible, these should slope slightly away from the house and other buildings. If you lower the grade at any point, do so by taking away sub-soil, not by skimming off good topsoil. You may raise the grade either by adding good topsoil or by removing the topsoil to a depth of eight or ten inches, filling in inferior soil and then replacing the topsoil.

Having taken care of the drainage and established grades, the next job is to prepare the seed bed. Dig, plow, or rototill deeply and add humus in very generous amounts.

On average soils a three-inch layer of manure, compost, leaf mold, natural humus, or peat moss is not too much. On sandy or gravelly soils more is advantageous. A lawn should last many years and you cannot get humus underneath, down where the roots are, once it is made.

If humus is not procurable in these amounts, delay sowing your permanent grass for a season. Grow a succession of green manure crops and turn each under when it is a foot or so tall.

The soil has been spaded and enriched with humus. Does it need lime? If in doubt, have a test made. Lawn grasses thrive best in soils that are neutral or very slightly acid. In most cases you are safe in applying 50 to 75 pounds of ground limestone (or thirty to forty pounds of agricultural lime) to each one thousand square feet. Fork or cultivate this into the upper four inches. Then let the soil settle for at least a week or two.

About ten days before you sow the lawn grass seed, spread a dressing of a complete fertilizer—a 5-10-5 is excellent. Or you may prefer a specially prepared lawn fertilizer. Spread it evenly and mix it thoroughly with the upper three or four inches of soil.

Early fall, after the heat of summer has passed, but well before killing frost, is the best time to sow permanent lawns. If you must sow in spring, do so early. You will need about four pounds of lawn seed mixture to each thousand square feet.

Unless you have some special reason for doing otherwise, use one of the specially prepared mixtures offered by seedsmen. For shaded or dry areas obtain special mixtures recommended for such places. But don't expect the impossible. You may not be able to have a lawn at all where shade is dense (tree roots rob the soil of food and moisture) or where the soil is just too dry. Perhaps groundcover plants will answer these problems for you.

Before scattering the seed, roll the area so the soil is firm underfoot and the surface is in a uniformly fine and even condition. Choose a calm day for sowing. Divide the seed into two equal amounts and sow one-half walking in one direction (lengthways) and the other walking in a direction at right angles (crossways) to this. Be sure to distribute the seed evenly.

After sowing, rake the seeds shallowly into the surface and roll the whole area.

Do not let the surface dry out after sowing, at least until the seeds are well germinated. If watering is necessary, be careful it is done gently so the surface is not eroded.

The first mowing should be done when the new grass is two inches high. Use a sharp mower and set it to cut at a height of one and a half inches. Be especially careful not to pull up the young plants. A light rolling following the first mowing and, if the weather is dry, a soaking with water is beneficial.

Renovating an Old Lawn. Provided basic soil conditions are good, much can be done to renovate an old lawn without remaking it. Late summer is the best time to do this but it is possible to get some improvement from a spring effort, if properly made.

First, find out why the lawn is poor. Lift a few squares of sod and dig to make sure the soil is sufficiently deep, reasonably good, and not waterlogged. Then check for insects—grubs that feed on the roots, chinch bugs and the like. If you think the soil is too acid, have a test made.

Correction of basic soil conditions that may be at fault, elimination of pests, and bringing the soil to an acidity-alkalinity range that approximates neutral on the pH scale are first essentials.

Once these problems are licked, you can tackle the elimination of weeds and the establishment of healthy turf with confidence.

Do not, however, expect young grass to compete successfully with well-established weeds. Six or eight weeks before you make your fall sowing of grass seed, begin a campaign to eliminate weeds. Make use of the selective weed killers that are available. These destroy many kinds without permanently damaging the grass. Handweed also.

Every effort to reduce the weed population is worthwhile.

When sowing time arrives, cut the grass to a height of one inch and rake out the clippings and any dead material. Loosen bare, packed areas with a fork and work humus or peat moss and a liberal sprinkling of bone meal into such spots. Minor depressions can be raised by top-dressing with rich soil.

Next, top-dress the entire lawn with a quarter inch layer of equal parts of humus and sandy topsoil, or peat moss and sandy topsoil to which bone meal (a pound to each bushel) has been added. Work this down into the grass with a broom.

Now apply a complete fertilizer, either one prepared especially for lawns or a regular garden fertilizer such as a 5-10-5. Use about three pounds of the latter to each hundred square feet, specially prepared fertilizers according to the manufacturer's directions. Spread it evenly and rake it.

You are now ready to seed. Use the best quality seed only. Two and a half pounds for each one thousand square feet is sufficient where there is a moderate amount of grass already.

After sowing, rake lightly and roll. Keep the soil evenly moist until the young grass is well up. Mow to a height of one and three-quarter inches but let it grow to a final height of two inches and allow it to go through the winter this long. Keep leaves from accumulating on your lawn.

Maintaining the Lawn. Maintaining an established lawn calls for rolling, mowing, weeding, watering, feeding, perhaps liming, and the control of diseases or pests.

Each spring, after the frost is out of the ground and while the soil is moist but not wet, roll with a medium-weight roller.

If your soil is deep, fertile, and rich in humus, the lawn will go through comparatively long dry periods with little harm. Even the best lawns will need watering in severe droughts, however. Don't wait until the grass is actually burned before watering. When water is needed, give enough to soak to a depth of four to six inches, then wait several days before giving more. Daily sprinkling is not good. It does no harm to water in sunshine.

What about Groundcovers?

Except in cultivated areas which are kept hoed or mulched, it is desirable to keep the surface of the soil covered with some kind of low vegetation. This keeps down weeds, prevents erosion, and protects the roots of trees and shrubs from extremes of heat and cold. If appropriately done, it also adds charm to the garden picture, showing off trees and shrubs and flowering plants to best advantage. Such greenery appears cool in summer and gives relief to the eye from the brighter colors in flower beds and borders.

Lawn is the most universally used green groundcover. For some purposes it is unsurpassed. No other groundcover that is practicable to maintain will stand the walking upon and the wear that grass will. If well cared for, no other groundcover is as generally admired.

Because of this, some gardeners make the mistake of attempting to solve all their groundcover problems by sowing grass seed. This just doesn't work. There are places where a lawn is certainly not the answer to the groundcover problem. In deep shade, for example, and on steep banks where it is almost impossible to use a lawn-

Ground cover cuts down on grass mowing, provides attractive, low-maintenance greenery.

Popular ground covers are *(left to right)* pachysandra, big blue lily-turf, lily-of-the-valley.

mower effectively. Also, where a perpetual battle to maintain grass has to be faced, even if you do succeed in establishing it, and in places where tree roots rob the soil of food and moisture.

In spots such as these try using some other groundcover. There are not many to choose from, it's true, but some very good ones do exist. There are plenty of low carpeting plants, of course, but few have the qualities of an acceptable groundcover.

Such a groundcover must provide a rather complete mantle for the soil surface. It must be perennial. It must be vigorous enough to maintain itself and keep down most weeds, but not so rampant that it crowds out its neighbors. It must require little maintenance.

Also, it should be inexpensive to purchase. This is a desirable quality indeed because it often takes a large number of plants to cover even a moderate area. But don't sacrifice quality and suitability for price considerations. All good groundcovers can be increased rather easily and most of them surprisingly quickly. So if you can't, or don't feel inclined to buy all the plants you need, then buy some.

Lay in a stock sufficient to plant part of the area you want to cover. And then begin a program of propagation. Within a year or two your stock will have increased manyfold.

Early spring and early fall are the best times to set out groundcover plants. If you are planting on steeply sloping land, the former is decidedly to be preferred, since there is less chance of erosion before the plants take hold. When planting such areas, mulch the surface with coarse compost or litter, just as a precaution.

Some groundcovers are evergreen, others die down during the winter. Most important in making a selection is to choose one highly adapted to the soil and situation you have to face. To look well, a groundcover must be in flourishing condition, not just hanging on.

These Are The Best Groundcovers

PACHYSANDRA (*Pachysandra terminalis*). Evergreen. Height 6 inches. Foliage rich green. Flowers white, rather inconspicuous. Forms a thick carpet and an interesting leaf pattern. Spreads slowly. Apt to "burn" in exposed places in winter. Set plants 6 or 7 inches apart. Propagate by division, cuttings, or root-cuttings. If in sun, needs fairly moist soil. Thrives in wide range of soils.

CREEPING MYRTLE (*Vinca minor*). Evergreen. Height 3 or 4 inches. Foliage deep, glossy green. Flowers blue or white, attractive. Forms a flat mat. Spreads rapidly. Set one-year or two-year old field-grown plants 12 inches apart each way. Propagate by division or cuttings. Grows well in poor soils.

PURPLELEAF WINTERCREEPER EUONYMUS (*Euonymus fortunei coloratus*). Evergreen. Height 9 to 12 inches. Foliage deep green becoming purple in winter. Flowers inconspicuous. Forms a somewhat loose spreading mat. May be kept more compact by shearing each spring. Spreads rapidly. Much less subject to scale insects than most euonymuses. Set plants 2 feet apart. Propagate by cuttings or by transplanting self-rooted stems. Thrives in wide variety of soils.

CARPET BUGLE (*Ajuga reptans*). Not evergreen. Height 2 or 3 inches. Foliage deep green or bronze. Flowers blue, attractive. Forms dense mat. Spreads rapidly. Set plants 9 to 12 inches apart. Propagate by division. Needs moderately moist soil.

DWARF LILY-TURF (*Ophiopogon japonicus*). Evergreen. Height 9 to 12 inches. Foliage deep green.

Flowers lilac, attractive. Forms dense turf. Spreads slowly. Set plants 10 to 12 inches apart. Propagate by division. Any ordinary soil.

BIG BLUE LILY-TURF (*Liriope muscari*). Evergreen. Height 9 to 12 inches. Foliage deep green or variegated with yellow. Flowers lilac. Forms dense turf. Spreads slowly. Set plants 10 to 12 inches apart. Propagate by division. Any ordinary soil.

MEMORIAL ROSE (*Rosa wichuraiana*). Not evergreen. Height 18 inches. Foliage medium-green. Flowers white, attractive. Forms tangled, thorny carpet. A vigorous grower, spreads fairly quickly. Set plants 3 to 6 feet apart. Propagate by cuttings. Not particular as to soil. Shear or prune back each year after blooming. Good for banks.

ROSE "MAX GRAF." Not evergreen. Height 1 foot. Foliage medium green. Flowers pink, attractive. A vigorous trailer. Spreads fairly quickly. Set plants 3 to 6 feet apart. Propagate by cuttings. Any well-drained soil. Shear occasionally if needed. Good for banks.

BEARBERRY (*Arctostaphylos uva-ursi*). Evergreen. Height 4 inches. Foliage dark green. Flowers white or pinkish. Berries red. Forms thick mat of trailing stems. Set plants one foot apart. Use pot-grown plants only. Propagate by cuttings. Needs acid soil. Thrives on sandy and gravelly soils.

MOSS PINK (*Phlox subulata*). Evergreen. Height 4 inches. Foliage light- to medium-green. Flowers white, lilac, pink, and red, showy. Forms dense mat. Spreads moderately fast. Set plants one to one and a half feet apart. Propagate by cuttings and division. Any well-drained soil.

CREEPING JUNIPERS (*Juniperus horizontalis,* and Bar Harbor juniper, Waukeegan juniper and some others). Evergreen. Height 12 inches. Foliage green or blue-green. No flowers. Form dense mats. Spread rapidly. Set plants 2 to 3½ feet apart. Propagate by cuttings. Any well-drained soil.

STONE-CROPS (*Sedum album, Sedum hybridum, Sedum rupestre, Sedum acre, Sedum sexangulare, Sedum stoloniferum* and others). Heights 4 to 9 inches. Foliage green. Flowers white, pink, red, or yellow. Form mats. Spread rapidly. Propagate by division or cuttings. Any well-drained soil.

ENGLISH IVY (*Hedera helix*) and
BALTIC IVY (*Hedera helix baltica*). Baltic ivy has smaller leaves and stands severe cold better than English ivy. Otherwise similar. Evergreen. Height 6 inches (climbs high if given support). Foliage dark green. Forms mat of trailing, rooting stems. Spreads rapidly. If exposed to sun or sweeping winds foliage "burns" badly in winter. Set plants 18 to 24 inches apart. Propagate by cuttings or by transplanting self-rooted stems. Needs moderately moist soil containing fair amount of humus.

LILY-OF-THE-VALLEY (*Convallaria majalis*). Not evergreen. Height to 6 inches. Foliage medium green. Flowers white, fragrant, highly attractive. Forms thick cover. Spreads slowly. Set plants 6 to 8 inches apart. Propagate by division. Needs rich, moist soil containing humus. Plants should be lifted, divided and replanted every few years.

EUROPEAN WILD GINGER (*Asarum europeum*). Evergreen 6 to 8 inches. Foliage dark, lustrous green, very handsome. Flowers inconspicuous. Forms neat cover. Spreads slowly. Set plants 8 or 9 inches apart.

Propagate by division and seeds. Needs rich, reasonably moist soil.

BARRENWORT (*Epimedium*—any kind). Not evergreen. Height 6 to 9 inches. Foliage green or bronzy green. Flowers white, pink or yellow; handsome. Forms a dense cover. Does not spread. Grows slowly. Set plants 10 to 12 inches apart. Propagate by division. Needs fairly moist soil rich with humus. Very choice.

Hedges—How to Plant and Maintain Them

Hedges are used to mark boundaries, provide backgrounds, insure privacy, and afford protection from wind, animals, and the neighborhood kids. They also, of course, give architectural character.

They may be sheared and strictly formal, lightly trimmed and semiformal, or untrimmed. Hedges are evergreen or deciduous, low or tall, wide or narrow.

No one plant offers all these variations. Decide upon the particular virtues you would like your hedge to have, then select the plant most likely to provide them. Consider not only what you want from the plant, but also what the plant needs to succeed. Can you supply the soil and situation that the plant you want must have?

Before you plant a hedge decide upon its ultimate height. The minimum width of a tall hedge at maturity is greater than that of a low hedge of the same kind. This width at maturity is something to consider, especially if you are planting along the boundary of neighboring property.

The wisest plan is to set hedges so that they will not intrude when fully grown. This means that the center of the hedge must be well inside the property line, the exact distance inside to be determined by the width of the hedge

Round-form hemlock hedges are green all year-round.

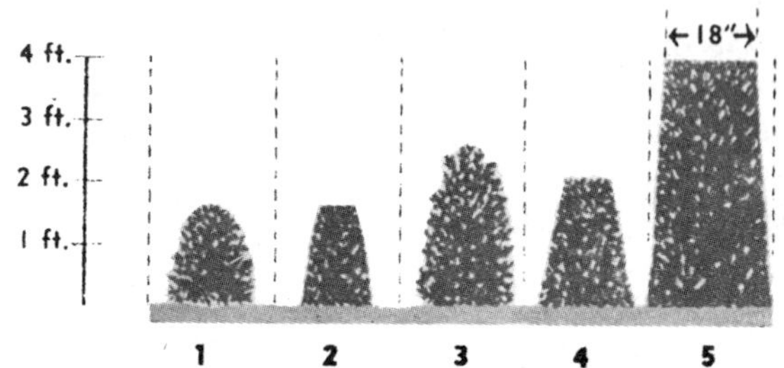

1. Plant only evergreens with leafy branches near the ground. 2. Trim lightly. 3. First-year growth. 4. Encourage bushiness by shortening growing shoots several times a season. 5. Shear hedges once or twice every year.

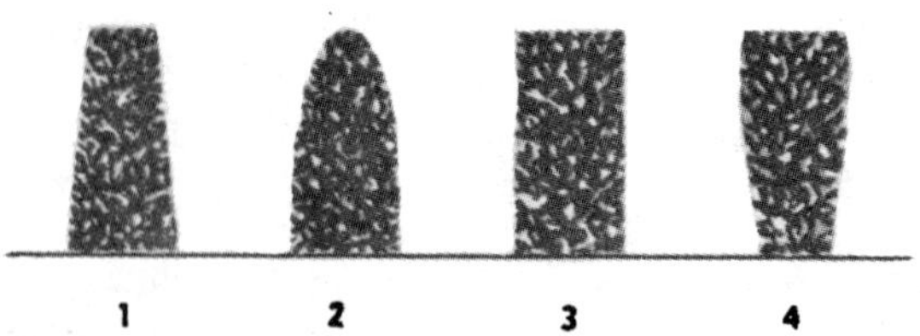

1. Good–tapering upwards. 2. Ditto. 3. Vertical sides are all right for privet and other strong-growing hedges. 4. Avoid this–the top should not be wider than the bottom.

at maturity, which in turn is dependent upon the kind of plant used and the height it reaches.

Having decided upon the kind of hedge you want, locate a source of supply. Young, vigorous, hedge plants are nearly always best. However, older plants can sometimes be used successfully for informal hedges and occasionally it is necessary to employ them to create immediate effects. Usually, plants one to three feet tall are preferred.

Planting. Plants in a hedge are crowded and need every help possible. Prepare the soil well. Dig a trench at least a foot deep and of ample width to take the roots without crowding. Spade plenty of manure or compost into its bottom. Mix humus and bone meal with the good topsoil packed about the roots.

Don't set hedge plants too far apart. For most deciduous kinds a foot apart in a single row or a foot and a half apart in a double row is best. Because of their cost it is often necessary to space evergreens at twice this distance.

Cut back newly-planted, deciduous hedges to within six inches of the ground. This takes courage but results in vigorous growth and a dense hedge well furnished to its base. Less severe treatment often results in an open bottom. After this initial pruning, don't trim the hedge again during its first season. The following spring cut it back to about a foot high and begin regular trimming. Prune newly-planted, evergreen hedges lightly.

Care of Hedges. Hedges need fertilizing, watering, spraying, and other care normally afforded shrubs and evergreens. They also need trimming (unless they are completely informal).

Never shape a hedge so that its top is wider than its base. Strong-growing types such as privet may have vertical sides but it is better to taper the hedge gradually to the top. The top may be flat, rounded, or pointed.

Trim formal hedges with hand or electric hedge shears. A knife or pruning shears is best for semiformal ones.

During the years the hedge is developing, shorten all strong-growing shoots several times during each season. This encourages bushiness and is especially important with evergreens.

Mature hedges need trimming once or twice a year only.

Deciduous Hedge Plants

GLOSSY ABELIA (*Abelia grandiflora*). Good sheared or unsheared. Semievergreen. 2 to 4 feet tall, 1 to 3 feet wide. Dark green. Pink flowers. In harsh climates winter kills, but the plant renews itself each summer. Sun or light shade.

FIVE-LEAVED ARALIA. (*Acanthopanax sieboldianus*). Good sheared. 2 to 5 feet high, 1½ to 3 feet wide. Medium green. Stems thorny, forming impenetrable hedge. Stands shade and city conditions well.

MENTOR BARBERRY (*Berberis mentorensis*). Good sheared or unsheared. Semievergreen. 2 to 5 feet tall, 1½ to 4 feet wide. Dark green. Stems thorny, forming impenetrable barrier. Stands heat and drought well.

JAPANESE BARBERRY (*Berberis thunbergii*). Good sheared or unsheared. 1½ to 5 feet tall, 1 to 3 feet wide. Light green. Variety *atropurpurea* reddish-plum colored. Flowers yellow. Berries red, long-lasting. Stems thorny, forming a good barrier. Stands shade, dryness, and poor soil.

BOX BARBERRY (*Berberis thunbergii minor*). Identical with Japanese barberry but lower and smaller leaves. 9 to 15 inches high, 6 to 9 inches wide.

TRUEHEDGE COLUMNBERRY (*Berberis thunbergii erecta*). Identical with Japanese barberry but more erect. Suitable for narrow hedges.

DWARF-WINGED EUONYMUS (*Euonymus alata compacta*). Good sheared or unsheared. 2 to 5 feet tall, 2 to 5 feet wide. Foliage green, brilliant red in fall. Stands some shade.

BEECH (American Beech, *Fagus grandifolia* and European Beech, *Fagus sylvatica*). Good sheared. 6 to 12 or more feet tall, 4 to 6 feet wide. Medium green. American Beech stands more cold than the European Beech, is somewhat more difficult to transplant. Both have surface root systems. Difficult to grow flowers near them.

COMMON BUCKTHORN (*Rhamnus cathartica*). Good sheared. 4 to 10 feet tall, 3 to 5 feet wide. Medium green. Thorny. Very hardy. Succeeds in shade and in dry places perhaps better than any other hedge plant.

GLOSSY BUCKTHORN (*Rhamnus frangula*). Not quite so dense as Common Buckthorn but more handsome. Otherwise similar.

PRIVET (Several kinds). Good sheared. 3 to 6 feet or more tall, 3 to 4 feet wide. Dark green. Quick growing. Stands shade. Amur Privet (*Ligustrum amurense*) is hardiest. California Privet (*Ligustrum ovalifolum*) has brighter foliage. Stands shade and other difficult conditions. Good under city conditions. Roots exhaust soil for some distance around. Difficult to grow flowers near.

Evergreen Hedge Plants

KOREAN BOXWOOD (*Buxus microphylla koreana*). Good sheared or unsheared. 2 to 2½ feet tall, 2 to 3 feet wide. Dark green. Slow growing. Hardier than Common Boxwood.

JAPANESE BOXWOOD (*Buxus microphylla japonica*). Identical with Korean Boxwood but taller. 3 to 4 feet tall, 2½ to 4 feet wide.

COMMON BOXWOOD (*Buxus sempervirens*). Good sheared or unsheared. 3 to 15 feet tall, 2 to 9 feet wide. Dark green. Slow growing. The choicest boxwood.

EDGING BOXWOOD (*Buxus sempervirens suffruticosa*). Identical with common boxwood but smaller. 1 to 2 feet tall, 1 to 2 feet wide.

ITALIAN CYPRESS (*Cupressus sempervirens*). Good sheared or unsheared. 4 to 12 feet or more tall, 2 to 3 feet wide. Dark green. For mild climates only.

JUNIPERS (Chinese Juniper, *Juniperus chinensis;* Red-cedar, *Juniperus virginiana*). Good sheared or unsheared. 4 to 12 feet or more tall, 3 to 4 feet wide. Green or blue green. Stand dryness well. Need full sun.

GLOSSY PRIVET (*Ligustrum lucidum*). Good sheared. 6 to 12 feet or more, 3 to 6 feet wide. Dark, glossy green. Suitable for mild climates only. Very handsome. Exhausts nearby soil of fertility and moisture. Difficult to grow flowers near.

PITTOSPORUM (*Pittosporum tobira*). Good sheared or unsheared. 3 to 6 feet tall, 3 to 5 feet wide. Dark green. Fragrant flowers. Suitable for mild climates only.

DOUGLAS FIR (*Pseudotsuga douglasii*). Good sheared. 6 to 12 feet or more high, 4 to 6 feet wide. Dark green.

JAPANESE YEW (*Taxus cuspidata* and varieties). Good sheared. 3 to 6 feet or more tall, 2 to 4 feet wide. Variety *nana* (often listed as *brevifolia*) best for low hedges. Dark green. Stands shade. One of the best hedges.

ENGLISH YEW (*Taxus baccata* and varieties). Similar to Japanese Yew but suited only for mild climates.

AMERICAN ARBORVITAE (*Thuya occidentalis*). Good sheared. 4 to 12 feet or more tall, 3 to 6 feet wide. Dark green. Stands some shade. Needs fairly moist soil.

HEMLOCK (Canada Hemlock, *Tsuga canadensis;* Carolina Hemlock, *Tsuga caroliniana*). Good sheared. 4 to 12 feet or more tall, 4 to 8 feet wide. Dark green. Stands light shade. Among the finest of hedge plants.

Vines in Variety

✤✤✤

You certainly have a place in your garden for a vine—to screen a porch, to clothe a pergola, to climb a chimney, to soften architecture, to relieve the monotony of wall or fence.

There is a vast number of vines from which you can choose. Select those best suited for your purpose.

To do this intelligently you must know something about how these plants climb. If you do not, you may make the mistake of planting a kind that permanently attaches itself, such as Virginia-creeper or Evergreen *Euonymus,* against a wooden house and have to tear it down next time the house is painted. Or you may court disappointment by planting a vine of restrained growth, such as the five-leaved akebia, in hopes that it will cover a tall chimney.

Stickers. Vines that cling or stick by aerial roots or by sucker-like discs should never be planted against supports that need painting. They belong only on masonry, brick or concrete walls, or against the trunks of trees. They are ideal for situations where tall climbers are needed, because they need no special supports.

Twiners. Twining vines twist themselves tightly around their supports by rotating the tips of their stems as they extend themselves. The important things to remember is that they cannot twine around objects that are too thick, trunks of trees for example. They need supports of lesser diameter such as stakes, wires, strings, or slender posts.

A few of the more vigorous, including wisteria and bittersweet, manage to scramble up tall trees, twisting two or three of their own stems to form sturdy upward extenders.

Some twiners rotate always in a clockwise direction as do the Japanese hop and the honeysuckle, but the majority, like the morning-glory, twine themselves from right to left, or counter-clockwise.

If you are starting the stem of a twining vine around a support be sure you wind it in the right direction, otherwise it must reverse itself before it can climb.

Tendril-Twiners. The sweet pea, cup-and-saucer vine and many others grip their supports by means of special organs called tendrils. These sensitive devices coil around strings, wires, brushwood, canes, and other objects of small diameter. They cannot take hold of thick supports. Similar in character are vines such as nasturtium which coil the stalks of their leaves around their supports.

Scramblers. Not all vines attach themselves. Climbing roses for example do not. They just scramble upwards, aided in the case of roses by their down-pointed thorns. But jasmines have no thorns. Neither do some others of their class. Scramblers weave their branches among each other and attain height in that way.

For convenience of culture we may consider vines as annuals and perennials. The annuals like other annual flowers are raised from seed each year. The perennials, if hardy to the locality, once established are there indefinitely.

Perennial Vines. Because perennial vines are luxuriant growers, give them the best you can in the way of soil preparation. Work the soil deeply. Add lots of compost o rotted manure and mix in a generous drenching of bone meal. Beware particularly of soil around the foundations of a house. It is apt to be poor sub-soil, covered with four or five inches of better soil. Excavate and discover what the conditions are before you plant.

Except in milder parts of the country plant in spring rather than fall, because the vines take hold of their supports quickly then and are less likely to be damaged by storms.

If you are planting English ivy, trumpet creeper or other vine that clings by rootlets or sucker discs, cut it down to within a few inches of the ground. In fact it pays to prune all perennial vines severely back at planting time. Set the plants as close to the support as possible.

Be sure that you water newly planted vines thoroughly during their first season or two whenever there is need for it. Beware of the soil drying if they are planted against a building that has an overhanging roof. Also give attention to watering established vines in dry weather. Don't do this merely when they are blooming.

Annual Vines That Soon Cover. Vines that you can grow and bloom in one summer are invaluable. You can do this with no more trouble or expense than buying a packet of seeds and sowing them in spring. Use them for temporary screens and backgrounds, to decorate fences and walls, and to give height and interest to the flower border. Some are fragrant and many provide excellent flowers for cutting. Such are the annual vines.

None cling by means of rootlets or sucker discs. All attach themselves either by tendrils, as does the sweet pea, or by twining stems, as does the morning glory. Therefore they must be provided with sticks, trellises, openwork fences, strings or wires.

Vines For Warm Regions. The milder the climate, the greater is the variety of perennial vines.

Most showy among the flowering ones are yellow allamanda, pink coralvine, pink, red and apricot *Bougainvillaeas,* yellow and orange *Bignonias, Beaumontia* (white

Few plants give the homey, softening, sentimental effect that vines provide—and in the main they are easy to grow.

flowers like Easter lilies), fragrant mignonette vine, white and red *Clerodendron* or gloryblower, lavender *Cryptostegia,* golden hibbertia, yellow and white jasmines, beautiful passion-flowers in red, blue and other colors, purple wreath or *Petrea* with lavender and purple flowers, scarlet rangoon creeper, cup of gold with huge chalices that change from cream to deepest gold, handsome lavender potato vines, sweetly fragrant, white *Stephanotis,* yellow orchid vine, and many others.

Perennial Vines

FIVE-LEAVED AKEBIA (*Akebia quinata*). Height 12 ft. or more. Flowers rather inconspicuous, fragrant. Foliage dark green, of refined appearance. Free of pests and diseases. Soil, rich. Position sunny, will stand light, shade, moderately mild climates (twiner).

DUTCHMAN'S PIPE (*Aristolochia durior*). Height 30 ft. Flowers insignificant. Foliage bold, handsome, forming a dense screen. Grows rapidly. Almost any soil and situation. Dies to ground each year (twiner).

TRUMPET VINE (*Campsis radicans*). Height 30 ft. Flowers red, orange or yellow. Summer. Foliage light green. Ordinary kind (Campsis radicans) attaches itself by aerial rootlets, Chinese kind (Campsis chinensis) has few or none. Rich moist soil and sunny position. Attracts humming birds. Prune back young growths fall or spring.

BITTERSWEET (*Celastrus orbiculatus*) Height 25-30 ft. Flowers inconspicuous. Fruits orange, decorative. Male plants do not fruit. Set male and female plants near each other. Difficult to transplant, cut back severely when transplanted. Soil, ordinary. Sun or light shade. Prune young growths severely fall, winter or spring. Much subject to infestations of scale insects (twiner).

CLEMATIS (Many Kinds). Height 6 to 15 ft. Flowers large or small, white blue, purple, pink or red. Among best are *jackmanii* (purple), *paniculata* (white, fragrant) and *montana rubens* (pink). First two may be pruned low, each spring, last should be lightly thinned only. Soil deep, cool, well drained, not acid. Keep mulched with compost or leaf mold. Position sunny, with roots shaded from sun. *Paniculata,* easiest to grow, is small flowered, blooms in fall. Seeds are attractive. Twines leaf stalks around supports.

CINNAMON VINE (*Dioscorea batatas*). Height 10-25 feet. Flowers small, white, fragrant. Foliage dark green. Grows rapidly, stems die to ground each winter. Any ordinary soil. Sun or shade (twiner).

EVERGREEN EUONYMUS (*Euonymus fortunei*). Height 30 feet. Handsome foliage. Fruits resembling those of bittersweet. Subject to infestations of scale insects. Any location. Ordinary soil, but in rich soil becomes established sooner. To encourage climbing provide supports from beginning. The hardiest evergreen vines (aerial rootlets).

ENGLISH IVY (*Hedera helix*). Height 50 feet or more. Evergreen. Handsome foliage. Flowers rather insignificant, fruits blue-black. Many varieties of which *Baltica* is hardiest. Likes rich, fairly moist soil. Thrives in shade, also in sun provided soil is not dry (aerial rootlets).

CLIMBING HYDRANGEA (*Hydrangea petiolaris*). 30 feet or more. Handsome foliage. Showy white flowers. Slow-growing when young. Plant against north or west-facing walls in deeply prepared rich soil. Excellent for sea-side. Both *Hydrangea petiolaris* and the rarer *Schizophragma hydrangeoides* are good. Prune back last year's growths winter or spring (aerial roots).

PERENNIAL PEA (*Lathyrus latifolius*). Height 6-7 feet. Flowers pink or white, resembling sweet peas but not fragrant. Rather difficult to transplant, always take ball of earth when moving them. Dislikes acid soil. Full sun. Very hardy (tendrils).

HONEYSUCKLE. Height 10-25 feet or more. Several kinds. Flowers white, apricot, red, etc., fragrant. Prune by thinning in spring. Soil ordinary. Position sunny. Halls honeysuckle which stands shade is apt to become a pest, difficult to eradicate (twiner).

CLIMBING ROSES (Many kinds). Height 6-20 feet. All colors except lavender, purple and blue. Fragrant. For culture see chapter on Roses (scramblers).

MOONSEED. Height 8 feet. Flowers inconspicuous. Fruits black, resembling small grapes. Foliage attractive. Dies down almost to ground each winter. Likes moist soil. Shade or sun (twiner).

BOSTON-IVY (*Parthenocissus tricuspidata*). Height 50 feet or more. Foliage handsome, brilliantly colored in fall. Often takes a year or two to begin climbing. Any ordinary soil. Sun or shade (discs on tendrils).

VIRGINIA CREEPER (*Parthenocissus quinquefolia*). Height 50 feet or more. Foliage handsome, brilliantly colored in fall. Any ordinary soil. Sun or shade. In damp, shaded places often is disfigured by mildew in fall (discs on tendrils).

SILVER LACEVINE (*Polygonum aubertii*). Height 25 feet. Flowers white in foamy masses. Foliage attractive. Prune back to live wood each spring. Any ordinary soil. Sun (twiner).

WISTERIA. Height 50 feet or more. Flowers blue, lavender or white, fragrant. Foliage attractive. Plants in shade or growing too vigorously often fail to bloom. Excessive vigor may be checked by root-pruning and by strict attention to summer pruning (see page 189). Plants raised from seeds often fail to bloom for many years. Get grafts from plants of known flowering ability. Somewhat difficult to transplant. Set plants from pots. Needs stout supports (twining).

Annual Vines

BALLOON VINE (*Cardiospermum halicacabum*). Height 5-10 feet. Flowers inconspicuous. Fruits decorative, resembling miniature balloons. Sow outdoors when all danger of frost has passed. Likes a warm sunny situation (tendrils).

BALSAM-APPLE (*Momordica balsamina*). AND BALSAM-PEAR (*Momordica charantia*). Heights 15-20 feet. Fruits curious, colorful, and ornamental. Foliage attractive, deeply lobed, rich green. Sow outdoors when trees begin to leaf or earlier indoors in pots and transplant later. Rich soil and sunny location desirable. Need plenty of moisture (tendrils).

BLACK-EYED SUSAN VINE (*Thunbergia alata*). Height 4-8 feet. Flowers orange, yellow, or white with purple-black throats. Tends to crawl on the ground. Good for window boxes, porch boxes, urns etc. Sow outdoors when soil is warm or indoors early and transplant later. Full sun and ordinary soil (twiner).

CANARY CREEPER (*Tropaeolum peregrinum*). Height 10-12 feet. Flowers clear yellow, attractively fringed.

Foliage deeply lobed, light green. Requires same treatment as nasturtium (twiner).

CARDINAL CLIMBER (*Quamoclit sloteri*). Height 15 feet. Flowers scarlet, resembling small morning glories, opening shortly after dawn, closing at nightfall. Foliage glossy green, attractively dissected. Culture same as for Cypress vine (twiner).

CUP-AND-SAUCER VINE (*Cobaea scandens*). Height 15-20 feet. Flowers large, bell-shaped, purple or white, good for cutting. Start in pots indoors 6 weeks before plants are to be set in open ground, set seeds on edge, scarcely cover them with soil. Avoid keeping too wet. Set plants in garden when weather is settled and warm. Likes full sun and warm, rich soil but will grow in partial shade (tendrils).

CYPRESS VINE (*Quamoclit pennata*). Height 10-15 feet. Flowers scarlet or white, star-shaped, open only at night and very early and very late in the day. Foliage green, fern-like, very dainty. Sow outdoors after soil has warmed up or indoors (twiner).

GOURDS. Height 8-12 feet. Fruits colorful and highly ornamental. Can be preserved for winter decoration indoors. Sow indoors in pots 6 weeks before ground is warm and weather is settled enough to transplant to open garden, or sow outdoors after all danger of frost is passed. Cutworms are apt to attack young plants. Rich soil best. Position sunny (tendrils).

HYACINTH BEAN (*Dolichos lablab*). Height 10 feet. Flowers white, lavender, purple, good for cutting. Fruits highly ornamental, white or purple. Sow outdoors after danger of frost has passed, or early indoors in pots and transplant later. Avoid disturbing roots. Full sun. Any reasonably good soil (twiner).

JAPANESE HOP VINE (*Humulus japonica*). Height 20-25 feet. Female plants have yellowish-green catkins. Foliage attractively lobed, often variegated with white. Fast grower. Sow early spring. Stands shade, heat and drought. Any reasonable soil (twiner).

MOON FLOWER (*Calonyction aculeatum*). Height 20 feet. Flowers large, white fragrant, open in the evening and at night only. Foliage heart-shaped, attractive. Soak seeds in tepid water for 24 or 48 hours before sowing. Sow indoors in pots 6 weeks before transplanting to open ground, which is done after weather is settled and warm. Soil ordinary. Full sun. Needs plenty of moisture when actively growing (twiner).

MORNING GLORY (*Ipomaea*). Height 8-20 feet. Flowers white, pink, red, purple, blue, and variegated. Leaves heart-shaped dark green. Sow directly outdoors in spring or start early indoors or in frame in pots and transplant to garden when danger of frost is over. Grows in any fair soil but responds to good conditions. Soak seeds in water for a few hours before sowing. Full sun (twiner).

NASTURTIUM. Height 6 feet. Flowers buff, yellow, orange red, maroon. Highly attractive. Foliage light green. Sow outdoors when ground is warm. Soil should not be rich in nitrogen otherwise excessive foliage develops at expense of blooms. Full sun. In many sections extraordinarily subject to infestations of aphids (twiner).

SCARLET RUNNER BEAN (*Phaseolus vulgaris*). Height 8-15 feet. Flowers scarlet. Beans and pods are edible before they are fully matured. Sow seeds outdoors after ground has warmed somewhat. Keep soil dryish until seedlings are well up. Plants require copious supplies of water during summer. Good soil and full sun (twiner).

SWEET PEA. Height 5-8 feet. Flowers all colors, except yellow. Fragrant, splendid for cutting. A cool weather annual, dies when hot, humid, weather comes. In favored sections sow outdoors in late fall, elsewhere at earliest date in spring it is possible to have the ground in condition. May also be started indoors or in frame in pots early and later transplanted. Soil deeply prepared, rich. Water freely during growing season. Fertilize generously. Keep all faded flowers picked (tendrils).

Annuals—for Quick Returns

✣✣✣

The quickest return on a minimum investment that your garden gives is provided by annuals. These plants bloom the year you plant them. You sow the seeds, care for the crop, enjoy the flowers, and discard the plants all within the space of a few months or even weeks. And next year you begin all over again. It's as simple as that.

Annuals are musts for the short-term garden. If you rent rather than own and don't want to spend too much on the garden, annuals are for you. If you want to improve your soil over a period of years by turning it each fall and adding humus, grow annuals. If you seek variety among cut flowers or want to brighten the garden during the summer try zinnias, marigolds, petunias, and other annual flowers.

No plants are easier to grow once their simple requirements are understood. Almost all need plenty of sun; a few stand light shade. All grow well in a freely-drained, fertile soil that would produce good vegetables. Some succeed in poorer soil.

Many can be sown outdoors. Others are usually started indoors or in a frame and are later transplanted to the garden.

Give annuals room to devolop. Keep them free of weeds, pests and diseases, water and stake them when necessary and they will reward you grandly.

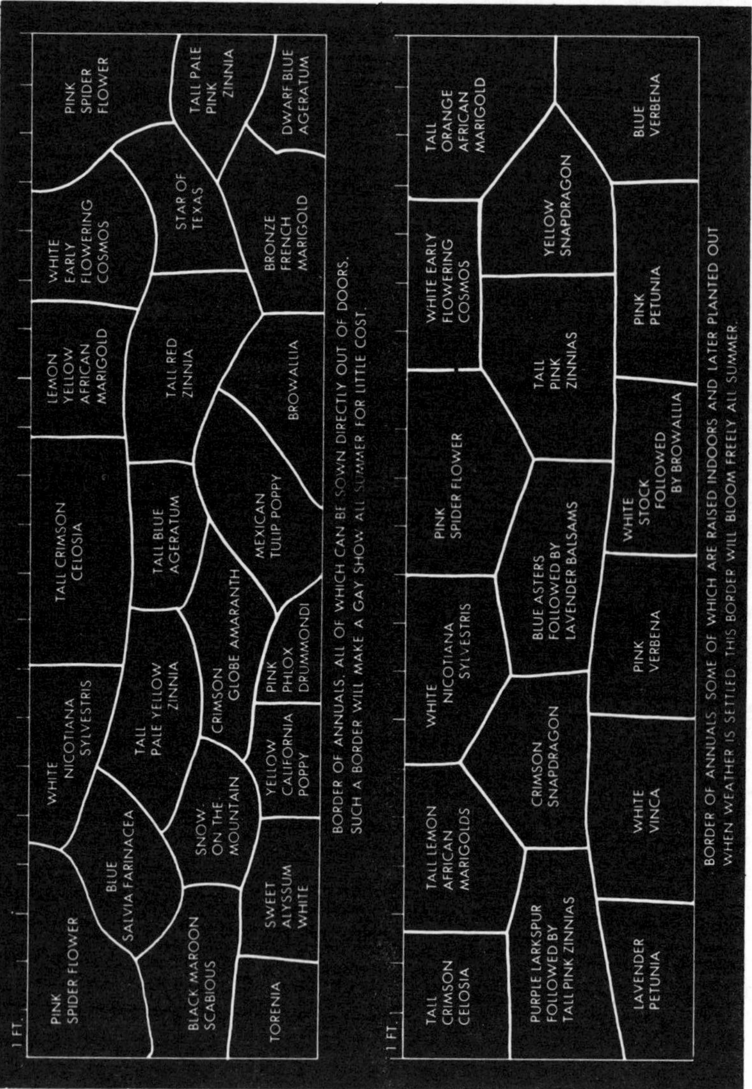

Avoid hard and regimented plans for annual beds. Here are two excellent layouts beginners can adapt.

It's important to select the kind of annuals best adapted to your purpose. Don't sow larkspurs or gaillardias, if what you want is an all-summer display because they bloom lavishly but briefly in early summer and die when the first real hot weather comes. Yet they are splendid as early summer cut flowers. On the other hand globe amaranth and begonias bloom all summer and are fine for garden display, but are of little use for cutting. And so it goes.

Sowing. There is no special trick to sowing annuals. The procedures are described in this book in "How To Sow Seeds." It is important to select appropriate dates. Sow those that you start indoors so that the plants are just ready to put out when the weather is warm enough to permit this. Do not let them get crowded and starved while awaiting transplanting. Amateurs commonly make indoor sowings too early. Avoid sowing so late, however, that your plants are undersized at setting-out time.

On the other hand they are apt to delay outdoor sowing too long. The seeds of many annuals should be gotten into the ground on the first occasion in spring when the soil is workable. With others, wait until danger from frost has passed. And in still other instances successive sowings to insure an extended season of bloom are desirable.

Care of Seedlings. From the time annuals sown directly out-of-doors break through the ground, give attention to surface cultivation. Keep down all weeds and maintain the top inch of soil in a loose condition. Never cultivate deeper than this. If you do, you will injure delicate feeding roots. Stir the soil each time rain packs it, not immediately after the rain ends but as soon as the soil has dried to the extent that it does not stick to shoes and cultivator.

You must thin the young plants too. Whether you sowed the seeds broadcast or in drills, the seedlings will (or should) come up more thickly than the mature plants are to be. There are maybe four times as many seedlings as you need in the area, or even more. Remove the surplus before they harm their neighbors by crowding.

If possible choose cloudy weather for thinning out. Don't remove all the surplus plants at one time. Spread the operation over three or four weeks. At the first thinning pull out the weakest seedlings of those that are beginning to crowd. When the plants left begin to touch thin again, once more take out the weakest (so far as you can make such a selection) and still leave those standing correctly spaced.

The ultimate spacing will depend upon the kind of annual you are thinning. A very approximate rule suggests that the plants should be spaced finally at distances equal to half their height. This is not exact because some kinds are naturally more spready than others. But it serves fairly well as a guide.

You may have sown some annuals of easily transplantable kinds such as asters or stocks in a seed bed outdoors, with the idea of moving them to their flowering quarters when big enough. This is a good plan if the place where they are to bloom is not ready at sowing time. Dig such plants up and transfer them when their second pair of leaves are well developed. Do not break the roots.

Planting. Cloudy weather is best for planting but you will not always be able to wait for this. Under exceptional conditions when you transplant in bright, hot weather you may have to shade the plants temporarily after they are moved. Usually this is not necessary. Water the plants thoroughly to settle the soil about their roots.

If plants are overgrown and "leggy," in most cases they will be improved if you pinch them back. Pinching back consists of cutting off or nipping off between the thumbnail and forefinger the tips of the growing shoots. This is successful only with such plants as petunias, snapdragons, and verbenas that form side branches.

Summer Care. After the plants are set out keep the surface soil cultivated regularly as advised for annuals sown directly outdoors.

Tall-growing plants will need support of some kind.

Staking should be done neatly and securely, and well before the plants grow crooked or have been damaged.

Unless you intend to collect your own seed, keep all faded flowers picked. This prolongs the blooming season. Seed production seriously drains the plant's energy. Sweet alyssum blooms better if sheared back when it begins to get straggly.

Supplementing Annuals. We may consider along with garden annuals such plants as geraniums, fuchsias, heliotropes, lantanas, coleus and alternanthera. Like recognized annuals these garden plants are set out in spring, decorate the garden for a single season, and in fall are dug up.

Grow these plants in pots. They transplant better from pots than from flats. Do not plant them outdoors until all danger of frost has passed and the weather has become settled and fairly warm. Their summer care is the same as for regular annuals.

Annuals with Attractive Colored Foliage

CASTOR OIL PLANT. Green or bronze. Sow outdoors when weather is settled. 3 feet apart.

DUSTY MILLER (*Centaurea gymnocarpa and Centaurea cineraria*). Gray. Sow early indoors and transplant or sow early outdoors.

AMARANTHUS (Molten Fire). Scarlet. Sow early indoors and transplant or sow early outdoors.

AMARANTHUS TRICOLOR (Josephs Coat). Red, yellow and green. Sow early indoors and transplant or sow early outdoors.

PERILLA. Red-purple. Sow early indoors and transplant or sow early outdoors.

Annuals: These Bloom from Seed the First Year

	Colors Available: White	Cream	Yellow	Orange	Brown	Red	Pink	Lavender	Purple	Blue	Suitable for Hot, Dry Places	Dies Out in Hot, Humid Weather	Will Stand Some Shade	Height in Inches	Approximate Distance Apart in Inches	Sow Outdoors Early	Sow Outdoors When Weather Is Settled	Short Blooming Season	Sow Indoors and Transplant for Early Bloom	Good as a Cut Flower	Sow June or Early July for Late Season Bloom	Sow Sept.-Nov. in Deep South	Difficult to Transplant. Sow Where to Bloom
Ageratum	✓						✓	✓		✓	✓		✓	6–24	8–12	✓			✓	✓			
Arctotis (African Daisy)								✓			✓	✓		15–20	9–12	✓			✓	✓			
Aster	✓	✓				✓		✓	✓	✓				9–36	9–12	✓			✓	✓			
Babysbreath	✓						✓							12–18	4–6	✓		✓		✓		✓	
Balsam	✓					✓	✓	✓					✓	9–18	9–10		✓		✓		✓		
Browallia	✓									✓				12–18	6–9	✓			✓	✓	✓		
Calendula		✓	✓	✓										9–18	8–10	✓			✓	✓	✓	✓	
California-Poppy		✓	✓	✓		✓	✓				✓			6–12	4–6	✓				✓		✓	✓
Calliopsis			✓	✓	✓	✓					✓	✓		12–30	6–9	✓		✓		✓			
Candytuft	✓					✓	✓	✓				✓		6–12	4–6	✓		✓	✓	✓	✓	✓	
Carnation	✓	✓	✓			✓	✓	✓	✓					8–18	6–10	✓			✓	✓		✓	
Celosia		✓	✓	✓		✓	✓							12–36	12–24	✓			✓	✓			
Chrysanthemum	✓	✓	✓									✓		12–18	8–10	✓		✓		✓			
Cornflower	✓					✓	✓	✓	✓	✓	✓		✓	12–30	8–10	✓		✓		✓		✓	
Cosmos	✓		✓	✓		✓	✓				✓			36–72	12–24	✓			✓	✓			
Four O'Clock	✓	✓	✓			✓	✓	✓			✓			20–24	15–18		✓						
Gaillardia			✓	✓		✓					✓	✓		12–18	6–9	✓		✓		✓		✓	
Globe Amaranth	✓					✓	✓	✓	✓					12–18	9–12	✓			✓	✓	✓		
Ice Plant	✓						✓				✓			4–6	4–6		✓						
Larkspur	✓					✓	✓	✓	✓	✓		✓		12–30	6–10	✓		✓		✓		✓	✓
Leptosyne			✓									✓		12–24	6–12	✓		✓		✓			
Linaria	✓	✓	✓			✓	✓	✓	✓	✓		✓		12–18	6–8	✓		✓		✓		✓	
Lobelia	✓						✓	✓		✓			✓	4–8	6–8				✓				

Love-in-a-Mist	✓							✓		✓		✓		8–12	6– 8	✓		✓		✓			
Marigold, African			✓	✓										24–42	12–24	✓			✓	✓	✓		
Marigold, French			✓	✓	✓									6–18	8–12	✓			✓	✓	✓		
Mexican Tulip-Poppy			✓											15–24	6– 9		✓			✓			✓
Mignonette		✓										✓		6–12	4– 6	✓		✓		✓			
Nasturtium		✓	✓	✓		✓					✓			9–15	6– 9		✓		✓	✓			
Nicotiana	✓					✓							✓	18–48	6–24	✓			✓		✓		
Petunia	✓	✓				✓	✓	✓	✓	✓	✓		✓	6–12	6– 9	✓			✓	✓			
Phlox	✓	✓	✓			✓	✓	✓	✓	✓	✓			6–12	4– 6	✓			✓	✓	✓	✓	
Poppy	✓	✓				✓	✓					✓		18–36	6– 9	✓		✓		✓		✓	✓
Portulaca	✓	✓	✓	✓		✓	✓	✓			✓			4– 5	2– 3	✓							
Rudbeckia (Blanket Flower)			✓	✓	✓							✓		20–24	8–10	✓		✓		✓			
Salpiglossis	✓	✓	✓	✓	✓	✓	✓	✓	✓			✓		24–34	6– 8	✓		✓	✓	✓			
Salvia	✓					✓	✓	✓		✓				24–42	10–15	✓			✓	✓			
Sanvitalia			✓								✓			3– 4	3– 4	✓							
Scabious	✓					✓	✓	✓	✓	✓				30–36	8–10	✓			✓	✓			
Snapdragon	✓	✓	✓	✓		✓	✓	✓						8–36	8–10				✓	✓		✓	
Snow-on-the-Mountain	✓										✓			24–36	10–15	✓				✓			
Spider Flower	✓						✓						✓	36–48	9–10	✓			✓				
Star of Texas			✓								✓			15–20	8– 9	✓			✓				
Statice	✓	✓	✓			✓	✓	✓	✓	✓	✓			12–24	6– 9	✓			✓	✓	✓		
Stock	✓	✓	✓			✓	✓	✓	✓	✓		✓		12–25	9–12	✓			✓	✓		✓	
Strawflower	✓	✓	✓	✓		✓	✓							24–36	9–10	✓		✓	✓	✓			
Sweet Alyssum	✓							✓						4– 8	3– 4	✓					✓	✓	
Sweet Sultan	✓	✓	✓					✓				✓		30–36	8–10	✓			✓	✓			
Sunflower		✓	✓	✓	✓									36–96	18–24		✓			✓	✓		
Tassel Flower						✓					✓			15–18	6– 9	✓							
Tithonia				✓										96	36	✓			✓	✓			
Torenia	✓								✓				✓	10–12	5– 7	✓			✓				
Verbena	✓					✓	✓	✓	✓	✓	✓			6– 9	8– 9				✓	✓			
Vinca	✓					✓	✓							9–15	8– 9				✓				
Wax Begonia	✓					✓	✓				✓		✓	8–12	8– 9				✓				
Zinnia	✓	✓	✓	✓		✓	✓	✓						9–36	6–10	✓			✓	✓	✓		

GIANT IMPERIAL STOCKS MEXICAN TULIP-POPPY CALENDULA SNAPDRAGON

These Take Two Years

✣✣✣

Biennials are plants that make substantial growth in their first year, and in their second, bloom and die. In addition to true biennials, gardeners find it advantageous to grow on a biennial schedule a few plants that are technically perennials. Such plants are considered here as biennials.

Some biennials are completely hardy and may be grown out of doors at all times. Others, in severe climates, need the protection of a cold-frame during the winter.

It is most important to sow the seeds at the right time. The sowing date should allow the plants to attain good size before winter, but not to become so large that they tend to run to flower in the fall, nor to become so leafy and soft that they are likely to be killed in winter.

Sowing dates vary in different parts of the country. Because a week or two one way or the other may make considerable difference, the best date to sow a particular biennial in your garden may differ by a week or more from the best date for a garden only a few miles away. Find the most favorable dates for your garden by experiment.

Biennials are all sown in the summer months. Sow them either in an outdoor bed or in a bed in a cold-frame. Make sure the ground is not likely to wash or erode if heavy rains come. The bed should be level. Take care that it is not under the drip of trees. In any case, prepare the soil very

When seedlings grow a second pair of leaves, transplant them to nursery beds. Keep the soil shallowly cultivated.

After ground freezes apply a light layer of loose material. In spring lift plants with a fork, plant in borders.

well and scatter the seeds in shallow drills spaced three or four inches apart.

After sowing, protect the seed bed with lath shades or with burlap tacked to light wooden frames to raise it a few inches above soil level. Such protection is necessary for shade-loving biennials such as fox-gloves and forget-me-nots and is desirable for others. Tiny seedlings are easily harmed by fierce summer sun. Do not keep glazed sash on cold-frames at this time of the year; shades alone are necessary.

The seed-bed must never become dry. Inspect it daily. When the young plants show above ground, gradually accustom them to stronger light if they are sun-loving kinds such as wallflowers. Begin by removing the shades both early and late and putting them in position only during the brightest part of the day. Then, after a few days, take them off altogether.

If the plants are kinds that need shade, leave the shades in place as long as necessary. The important thing is not to shade so heavily that the plants become "drawn" or "leggy" or weak. Keep the seed-bed weeded and lightly cultivated.

This sowing-in-a-special-seed-bed technique is practically essential to success in raising biennials. I have seen many beginners sow their biennials in a patch in the perennial border or in the front of the shrub border or in some other place among other plants. It never works.

Not only must they have a good seed-bed, but you must also arrange for nursery-beds (or cold-frames) on which to grow them. Biennials are grown almost to full size before they are transferred to the locations where they are to bloom. Rarely if ever will they develop satisfactorily if they are set out among other plants when small.

Biennials bloom in spring and early summer, and then die.

GARDEN BIENNIALS

CANTERBURY BELLS. For borders and cut flowers. Height 3 to 4 feet. Blooms in June-July. White, pink, lavender, purple. Sow in June. Space 12 by 9 inches in nursery beds. Full sun.

ENGLISH DAISIES. For edgings and beds. Height 6 inches. Blooms in early spring to beginning of hot weather. White, pink, red. Sow in June. Space 6 inches each way in nursery beds or cold-frames. Full sun.

FORGET-ME-NOTS. For beds and borders. Height 6 to 9 inches. Blooms in spring. Blue, white, pink. Sow in late July. Space 8 inches apart in nursery beds or frames. Needs light shade when growing. Stands full sun at flowering time.

FOXGLOVES. For borders and cut flowers. Height 3 to 6 feet. Blooms in June-July. White, pink, purple. Sow in June. Space 15 by 10 inches in nursery beds. Sun or light shade when in nursery beds; lightly shaded for flowering.

HOLLYHOCKS. For borders. Height 5 to 7 feet. Blooms in July. White, yellow, pink, red, maroon. Sow in June. Space 15 by 12 inches in nursery bed. Full sun. When grown as biennials they are not much affected by rust disease.

HONESTY. For borders and cutting. Blooms in May. Attractive seed pods follow. White, purple. Sow in June. Space 12 by 9 inches apart. Light shade.

MULLEINS (*Verbascum*). For borders. Height 2 to 6 feet. Blooms in early summer. White, pink, purple, yellow. Sow in June. Space 12 by 10 inches in nursery beds. Light shade.

PANSIES. For beds and borders. Height 6 inches. Blooms in spring until coming of hot weather. All colors and mixtures except bright red. Sow in late July or early August. Space 6 to 8 inches apart. Light shade. Will stand full sun in flowering quarters.

ROSE-CAMPION (*Lychnis coronaria*). For beds and borders. Height 2 to 3 feet. Blooms in June-July. Crimson. Foliage white-wooly. Sow in June. Space 12 by 10 inches in nursery beds. Full sun.

SWEET WILLIAMS. For beds, borders and cutting. Height 1 to 2 feet. Blooms in late spring. White, pink, red, variegated. Sow in June-July. Space 12 by 9 inches in nursery beds or cold-frames. Sun or light shade.

Perennials for Permanence

Hardy perennials are the backbone of the flower garden. They come in immense variety. Some, such as day lilies, are so good-natured and tenacious in their attachment to life that the most inexperienced beginner cannot fail with them. Others, including the rarer primroses and the New Zealand forget-me-not, are so difficult to satisfy that it is unusual for the most skilled gardener to bring them to bloom. Between these extremes is a vast number of easy-to-grow and reasonably easy-to-grow kinds, from among which you can select those that suit your needs.

When choosing perennials consider the purposes for which you need them. For cut flowers? To plant alone in a bed? As a group in a border or by the waterside? As an edging?

What height should the plants be? Upright or spreading? When do you want them to bloom?

The Perennial Border. Let's suppose you want to make a perennial border, which is a popular way of using these plants. You wish a variety of flowers you would like to bloom from spring to fall and you want pleasing color arrangements.

First choose the location. The ideal has soil that is deep, rich and well drained, receives sunshine practically the whole day (light shade from the hottest mid-day sun would

Columbine.

Iris.

Primula.

Fragrant onion.

Blackberry lily.

Cottage pink.

Nepeta nervosa.

Butterfly weed.

Stokes aster.

Monarda.

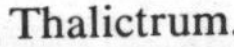

Thalictrum.

be splendid), and is sheltered from sweeping winds. You may have to settle for less. But at least strive.

Don't attempt a perennial border in unimproved subsoil from a cellar excavation, in soil that is exhausted of nourishment and moisture by nearby trees, or in dense shade. If your ground is waterlogged, drain it or try some of the common bog plants.

Locate your border so that it fits pleasingly into the garden plan, so it can be seen from the terrace or from one of the principle windows. It can be a boundary to the lawn, or part of a formal garden.

If possible provide a background—a hedge, a wall, or a fence. Without such support a border is rarely as effective as with it. Walls of all kinds are good, especially if partially vine-clothed. Hedges, particularly evergreen hedges, are excellent except that greedy rooting kinds (such as privet) so rob the soil that perennials planted close to them suffer. Periodic root pruning of the hedge and additional fertilization and watering for the perennials is a partial answer. Informal backgrounds of evergreens or shrubs can be lovely.

Borders may be straight or curved or undulating but they must end somewhere. Just as backgrounds are important so are logical endings, and here again walls, fences, hedges, or well-chosen groups of evergreens or shrubs suggest themselves.

Make the border not less than six feet wide. Eight or nine is better if tall plants are used. Long borders in the largest gardens should not exceed twelve feet in width.

Before you plant, fix up the soil. Once the plants are in you won't be able to do much more than tickle its surface for three or four years. So go to town at the beginning. If it is very poor, remove the soil to a depth of at least a foot and replace it. Or crop it for a couple of years with annuals and improve it between crops by turning it and mixing in lots of humus. This will delay the planting of perennials but the results should be worth it.

Most perennials bloom for a comparatively short season. When not flowering, their foliage takes up space, and needs light and air, while their roots need moisture and fertility. Interplanting of kinds that bloom at different seasons is helpful but is limited by these circumstances.

If you settle for less than a season-long riot of color, you can have a good perennial border. Here's how. Use a few reliable standbys and repeat these, in different colors perhaps, along the border.

See that these basic items include kinds that bloom at different seasons and types that reach different heights.

In June, for example, clumps of peonies, irises, and pinks may give character to your border. In high summer the main show might be phlox, day lilies, and veronicas. For fall color rely upon asters and chrysanthemums in varying colors and heights. Between groups of these basic plants set others to give diversity and interest. Choose kinds that bloom for a long time when possible. Plant hardy bulbs also: for spring, daffodils, tulips, hyacinths and others; for summer, the hardy amaryllis.

Planting and Replanting. By following the above suggestions you will have the best possible border of a type that does not need new planting each year. This does not mean that once planted the garden will go on forever without replanting. Perennials grow, exhaust the soil, and crowd their neighbors. Make over your border every third or fourth year. Dig up the plants. Fix the soil by turning it deeply and conditioning it with humus, lime if needed, and fertilizer. Replant after dividing those perennials that need such treatment. If this is too much to do at one time, then make over a third or fourth of the area each year so that the entire border is done every three or four years.

You may wonder when the border should be remade. You have read that irises should be transplanted in early summer, peonies in late summer, phlox in fall, and anemones in spring. How then can you remake a border containing all these at one time? The truth is that these recommended planting seasons are rules for perfection. Apply them if you have beds or borders given over to one kind of plant or if you are buying new plants that come as small divisions and have been out of the ground for some time. But in fall, after the first frost, and while the ground is still warm enough to encourage new roots, you can transplant almost any perennial in your own garden successfully. And that's the time to remake your border. Start as early as possible.

Although any perennial can be transplanted successfully in early fall, there are a few that prefer not to be moved at any time. It is better to dig around these and leave them undisturbed.

After the plants are lifted, heel them in (that is, plant them very closely together in rows) in some out of the way corner while the soil improvement is in progress. Be sure to label them carefully. If possible complete the soil work rapidly and replant immediately. If it is not possible to do this in time for the plants to make new roots before the ground freezes up, delay replanting until spring. The plants will be all right heeled in if the soil where they are is well drained. Cover them with leaves, salt hay or evergreen branches over winter. Or, if you prefer, keep them in a cold-frame.

Before you plant make a plan. It's easy to do this on graph paper. Arrange the plants in irregular groups or drifts. Use occasional single specimens of bold subjects such as peonies and gas plants; in most cases set three, five, or more plants of a kind together.

At replanting time divide the plants that need it, and most will. When planting, spread the roots and work the soil well in between them. Don't set the plants too high or too low. In nearly all cases their crowns should be about an inch below the surface. Make the soil firm about the roots. No watering is necessary unless the soil is really dry, which is unlikely to be the case. Take care to keep the soil surface neat and level, and cultivate it lightly when the planting is finished. After the ground has frozen apply a winter covering.

Care of Perennials. Routine work with perennials consists of removing the winter covering when spring arrives. Don't do this too early. Better leave the covering in position until you are sure winter has departed. Don't leave it in place so long that the plants are harmed, however. If the covering is heavy remove it gradually. Choose weather that is dull and moist rather than sunny and windy for this task.

Keep the soil cultivated regularly or mulch with leaf mold, compost, peat moss, or other suitable material when the weather begins to get really warm. Don't mulch too early. Water in dry weather. Soak the soil to a depth of six inches or more. Then give no more until it is dry again. In hot weather this may be in four or five days. Do not hesitate to water in sunshine if the plants are in need of moisture.

Other Ways of Using Perennials. The perennial border is a favorite garden feature. Perennials can also be grown in beds by themselves, as edgings, occasionally as solitary specimens, and in other ways. Details of their planting and care are the same. If you need cut flowers in quantity establish a special cutting garden and there line your perennials out in rows as you would shrubs in a nursery or vegetables in the kitchen garden. In this way you can grow many other flowers with the same effort.

Propagation. Division is the simplest way to increase most perennials. Cuttings and root-cuttings are used for some. Seeds, sown in a cold-frame or out-of-doors in the same way as biennials, are successful with many, but highly developed garden varieties cannot be propagated in this way. Progeny raised from their seed is almost always very inferior. If a perennial is a named variety, don't raise it from seed.

A SELECTION OF GOOD PERENNIALS

Blooming times of the early season ones will be earlier in the South and later in the Northernmost parts of the country than indicated here.

THESE BLOOM APRIL-MAY

Name	How to Propagate	Color	Height in feet	Remarks
Anemone pulsatilla *(Pasque Flower)*	seed	lavender	1	Attractive in seed as well as in bloom.
Arabis albida *(Rock Cress)*	seed, division, cuttings	white	1	The double-flowered kind is especially good. Single flowered kind can be raised from seed.
Brunnera macrophylla *(Forget-me-not Anchusa)*	seed, division	blue	2	Good for shade and moist soils.
Euphorbia myrsinites	seed, division	yellow	1	
Viola odorata *(Sweet Violet)*	division	purple, violet, white	½	Needs fairly moist humusy soil and location that is shaded and cool in summer. North side of wall is good place.

THESE BLOOM MAY

Name	How to Propagate	Color	Height in feet	Remarks
Alyssum saxatile *(Basket-of-Gold)*	seed	yellow or lemon	1	Old plants are not easy to transplant. Easy to raise young ones.
Amsonia tabernaemontana	seed, division	pale blue	1½	Good for partial shade.
Anchusa azurea *(A. italica)*	root-cuttings, divisions, seed	pale blue	4	Some individuals are much better than others. Select the best seedlings and propagate by root-cuttings or division.
Aquilegias *(Columbine)*	seed	white, yellow, blue, red, lavender	2-4	Short lived. Raise a few plants from seed each year. Likes light shade.
Armeria maritima lauchneana *(Thrift)*	division	rose-crimson	½	Good for edgings. Does well in hot, dry places. Good for Seaside.
Cerastium tomentosum *(Snow-in-Summer)*	seed, division	white	1	A lover of sunshine.
Convallaria majalis *(Lily-of-the-Valley)*	division	white	¾	Needs shade and rich fairly moist soil.
Dicentra spectabilis *(Bleeding Heart)*	division	pink	2-3	Foliage dies down middle of summer.
Doronicum *(Leopardbane)*	division	yellow	1½	
Helonias bullata *(Swamp-pink)*	division	pink	2	Likes moist or wet soil.
Iberis sempervirens *(Evergreen Candytuft)*	seed, division	white	¾	Shear back lightly after flowering.
Iris (many kinds)	division	white, yellow, blue, purple	½-3	See Chapter "How to grow Irises."
Linum *(Flax)*	seed	white, yellow, blue	1½	Need full sun. Stand dry soils. Flowers drop early in afternoon.
Mertensia virginica *(Virginia Bluebell)*	seed, division	blue or pink	2	Foliage disappears in summer.
Phlox divaricata *(Blue Phlox)*	seed, division	blue, purple-blue	1	Does well in light shade.
Phlox subulata *(Moss-pink)*	division, cuttings	white red, pink magenta	½	Needs full sun. Stands dry soil.
Polemonium reptans	division	blue	¾	Good carpeter.

Name	How to Propa-gate	Color	Height in feet	Remarks
Polygonatum multiflorum *(Solomons-Seal)*	division,	white,	3	Good for shade.
Primula *(Hardy Primroses)*	seed, division	yellow, orange, pink, red, blue	½-3	Require moist soil rich with humus, and light shade.
Trollius *(Globe Flower)*	seed, division	yellow, orange,	1-3	Best in deep, rich moist soil.

THESE BLOOM JUNE

Name	How to Propa-gate	Color	Height in feet	Remarks
Allium tuberosum *(A. odorum)*	seed, division	white	2½	Fragrant.
Aster alpinus "Goliath"	seed, division	blue-purple	1	
Campanula glomerata	division	purple	2½	
Astilbe many kinds *(Spireas)*	division	white, red, pink	2	Need moist soil. Will stand light shade.
Campanula persicifolia in variety *(Peach leaved Bell Flower)*	seed, division	white, blue	2-3	
Belamcanda chinensis *(Blackberry-lily)*	seeds	orange spotted with black, orna-mental seeds	2-3	Full sun.
Chrysanthemum coccineum *(Pyrethrum or Painted Daisy)*	seed, division	red, pink	2	Need light well drained soil.
Coreopsis lanceolata grandiflora *(Tickseed)*	seed, division	yellow,	3	
Delphinium hybrids	seed	lavender, purple, blue, white	6	Usually short-lived. Raise new plants every year or two.
Dianthus plumarius *(Cottage Pink)*	seed, cuttings	red, white, pink	1	Needs full sun. Fragrant.
Dianthus gratianopolitanus *(D. Caesius)* *(Cheddar Pink)*	seed, cuttings	red, white, pink	1	Needs full sun. Fragrant.
Dictmnus albus *(Gas Plant)*	seed, division	white, pink, red	3	Resents transplanting. Leave undisturbed if possible.
Filipendula hexapetala *(Dropwort)*	division	creamy-white	3	Low ferny foliage.
Gaillardia *(Blanket Flower)*	seed	yellow, orange, red	2	
Geum *(Avens)*	seed	yellow, orange, red	1½-3	
Gypsophila paniculata *(Babys-Breath)*	seed, grafting	white	3	Needs sun. Do not transplant oftener than necessary.
Helenium Hoopesii *(Helen's Flower)*	division	yellow	1½	
Hemerocallis *(Daylily)*	division	yellow, lemon, orange deep red	2-3	Easy anywhere. Stand light shade.
Heuchera *(Alum-root)*	division	white, pink, red	1-2	
Iris (several kinds)	division	all colors except red	2-3	See "How To Grow Iris."

Name	How to Propagate	Color	Height in feet	Remarks
Lychnis Viscaria *(German Catchfly)*	seed, division	magenta	1½	Difficult color to place. Use near whites or where green predominates.
Nepeta Mussini	division, cuttings	pale blue	2	Needs sun. A good edging plant.
Nepeta "Souvenir de Andre Chaudron" *"Blue Beauty"*	division, cuttings	blue	2	Needs sun.
Oenothera missouriensis *(Ozark Evening Primrose)*	division	yellow	1	Full sun.
Paeonia (Peony)	division	red pink white,	2-3½	Sun or light shade.
Papaver orientale *(Oriental Poppy)*	root-cuttings	pink, red white	3	Foliage dies down in summer. For full sun and well drained soil.
Phlox carolina *(P. suffruticosa)*	division, cuttings	white, pink,	2½	Sun or light shade.
Polemonium coeruleum *(Jacobs Ladder)*	division	blue	2	
Thalictrum aquilegifolium *(Meadow-rue)*	seed, division	white to purple	3	
Thermopsis caroliniana	seed	yellow	5	Like a tall yellow lupine.

THESE BLOOM JULY

Name	How to Propagate	Color	Height in feet	Remarks
Achillea Ptarmica *"The Pearl"*	division	white	2	
Althea rosea *(Hollyhocks)*	seed	white, yellow, pink, red	6	These are better grown as biennials. When kept as perennials are disfigured by rust disease.
Betonica grandiflora *(Betony)*	division seed	rose purple	2-3	
Chrysanthemum maximum *(Shasta Daisy)*	division	white	2-3	Needs full sun and rich soil. Divide every two years.
Clematis davidiana	seed, division	blue	3	These are bush types.
Clematis mandchurica	seed, division	white	3	These are bush types.
Echinops Ritro *(Globe Thistle)*	seed, division	blue-gray	4	
Erigeron speciosus *(Fleabane)*	division	lavender	2	
Hemerocallis *(Daylily)*	division	yellow, orange, brown	2-3	Easy. Stand light shade.
Monarda didyma *(Bee-balm)*	seed, division	white, pink, scarlet	2-3	Stands moist soil and some shade.
Penstemon barbatus *(Beard-Tongue)*	seed, division	scarlet	3	
Platycodon *(Balloon-flower)*	seed, division	blue, or white	2	
Rudbeckia *(Coneflower)*	seed, division	yellow, red purple, or white	3-6	
Stokesia cyanea *(Stoke's Aster)*	seed, division	blue, white	1	Needs sharp drainage.
Thalictrum glaucum *(Meadow-rue)*	division	yellow	3-4	Blue-grey foliage, fragrant.
Valeriana officinalis *(Garden Heliotrope)*	seed, division	pink, white, lavender	4	Fragrant.

Name	How to Propagate	Color	Height in feet	Remarks
THESE BLOOM AUGUST				
Acenitum *(Monkshood)*	division	blue, or blue-white	4	Appreciate a little shade and rich, moderately moist soil.
Anemone hupehensis	seed, root-cuttings	lavender, rose-	2	Do not transplant oftener than necessary.
Asclepias tuberosa *(Butterfly-weed)*	seed	orange	2-3	Difficult to transplant.
Eryngium *(Sea-holly)*	seed	blue	2-2½	
Hosta *(Plantain-lily)*	division	white, lavender, blue	1-2	Good for shade.
Hibiscus *(Rose-mallow)*	division	white, pink, red	4-5	Needs full sun and moist soil.
Liatris *(Blazing Star)*	seed, division	pink, white	3-5	
Phlox paniculata *(Hardy Phlox)*	division, cuttings	white, pink, red	3-4	Much subject to disease.
Salvia Pitcheri	seed, division	blue	4	
THESE BLOOM SEPTEMBER				
Aconitum *(Monkshood)*	division	blue-violet	5	Stand light shade, fairly moist soil. Do not transplant unless necessary.
Anemone *(Japanese Anemone)*	division, or root-cuttings	white, pink, red	2-4	Moist soil, light shade. Do not transplant unless necessary.
Aster *(Michaelmas Daisy)*	division	white, lavender, pink, red, blue	1-6	
Eupatorium coelestinum *(Mist-Flower)*	seed, division	blue	3	Comes up very late in spring.
Helianthus multiflorus fl. pl. *(Perennial Sunflower)*	division	yellow		Blooms resemble those of double dahlias.
Helenium *(Helen's Flower)*	seed, division	yellow, copper-red	3-5	
Hosta *(Plantain-lily)*	division	white, lavender,	1-2	Good for shade
Physostegia "Vivid" *(False Dragonhead)*	division	white pink, red	2-4	Spreads rapidly.
Sedum spectabile	division, cuttings	pink, red	2	For full sun and dry soils.
THESE BLOOM OCTOBER				
Chrysanthemum arcticum	division, cuttings	white	2	
Chrysanthemum, hardy	division, cuttings	white cream, yellow, bronze, red	2	One of the most effective fall flowers.
[illegible]	division,	white	2-4	Give rich soil, full sun and divide and replant each spring.
[illegible]	division, seeds	lavender, spotted purple,	2-3	Rich woodsy soil and shade.

Beauty from Bulbs

The group of plants that the gardener knows as bulbs is a vast one. Not all are dealt with here but a great many of the best and most popular are. You will find others discussed in the chapter on Rock Gardens.

The requirements of bulbs are various but one thing is certain: most are harmed if fresh manure is near them. Because this is well known, many beginners are scared about fertilizing at all. This is a mistake. Bulbs respond to intelligent fertilizing as do other plants. Some, such as cannas, elephants ears, and crinums are big feeders.

Nearly all revel in compost, leaf mold, and similar mild forms of humus. Mix these liberally with your soil. I know of no bulb that does not find bone meal to its liking. Use it at the rate of half a pound to a pound for each square yard, and work into soil.

Stagnant water is disastrous to most bulbs. They must have good drainage. Yet, they require liberal supplies of moisture while growing, whenever their leaves are green and above ground.

The way tulip bulbs are planted provides basic bulb-planting techniques. First step in preparing the soil is to spread bone meal on it. Next, fork the bed over deeply, mixing the bone meal thoroughly with the soil. Then tread on the bed to consolidate it, and rake it to establish a fin[illegible] consistency, and a finished grade. Now take the bulbs[illegible]

Oxalis bowieana.

Tuberose. Ornithogalum arabicum. Caladiums.

Spanish bluebells. Daffodils. Autumn crocus.

place them six inches apart on the surface (unless other spring-flowering plants are to be set between them). Don't line them up like soldiers, but in a soft, informal arrangement. Take a trowel, lift the first bulb from its place, and stab trowel deeply into the bed, drawing the soil up and toward you, holding the trowel like a dagger, concave side facing you. Place the bulb in loose soil about a hand's depth down, and press it in. Fill the hole and press the earth down firmly, finishing it off level and neat with the edge of the trowel. Don't use a dibble in planting bulbs as they may stick part way down in the narrow hole instead of resting firmly at the bottom.

Spring-flowering bulbs for fall planting. These hardy bulbs are all easy to grow. See that the soil is deeply prepared and adequately drained. Plant at the right depth and at the right time. Bulbs planted in grass need no additional protection during winter. If planted in bare ground, most benefit from a mulch of leaves, litter, salt hay, or evergreen branches applied after the ground has frozen. If you put the mulch on too early you invite mice to take up winter quarters. Do not let bulbs suffer from drought at any time when they have green leaves showing. Never remove foliage until it has yellowed.

HYACINTH. For formal beds and borders. Group in front of a perennial border. Very fragrant. All colors. Good when planted near or interplanted with other spring-blooming plants such as arabis, *Alyssum saxatile,* pansies, English daisies, and forget-me-nots. Available in several grades. Buy "bedding" size (17-18 centimeters or 2¼ inches in circumference). Lift after foliage dies; the bulbs bruise easily. Handle carefully. Store one layer deep in cool, dry, airy place. Plant in October. Hyacinths need sun and light and rich, extremely well-drained soil.

SPANISH AND ENGLISH BLUEBELLS. For grouping in borders. For woodland gardens. For cutting. Blue,

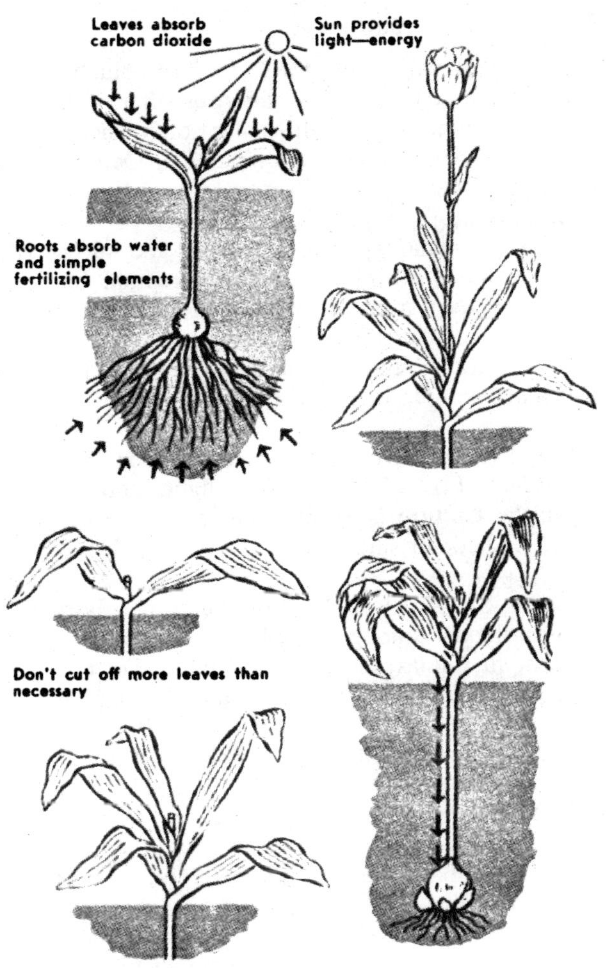

As the plant emerges into the sun its leaves make food from water and carbon dioxide while the roots absorb water and nutrient elements. After the plant blooms, do not remove leaves unnecessarily. Whether or not the plant blooms next year depends on the amount of food made by the leaves and stored away underground in the blub.

pink, and white. Fragrant. Spanish bluebell (*Scilla campanulata*) is more vigorous than the English (*Scilla nutans*). Lift and replant only when obviously overcrowded. Plant in September-October. Deep, reasonably moist soil. Shade.

CROCUS. For naturalizing in grass and along fringes of shrubbery. For growing in perennial border. All colors except red and pink. Lift and replant only if overcrowded or if bulbs work their way to the top of the ground. Plant in September-October. Light, well-drained soil preferred. Sun or light shade.

CAMASSIA. For woodland gardens. For grouping in borders. For cutting. White, light, and deep blue-purple. Culture is exactly the same as Spanish bluebells. Shade or sun.

SUMMER SNOWFLAKE. For perennial border. For naturalizing among shrubbery. For cutting. White. Plant in fall as soon as obtainable. Do not lift and replant unless overcrowded. Sun or light shade.

SNOWDROP, GRAPE-HYACINTH, SQUILL (*Scillas*), GLORY-OF-THE-SNOW, WINTER ACONITE. For naturalizing beneath shrubbery. For perennial border. For rock-gardens. Snowdrops are white; grape hyacinths are blue and white; squills and glory-of-the-snow are blue, pink, and white; winter aconites are yellow. Easy and permanent. Plant in fall as soon as you can obtain them. Sun or light shade. Winter aconite needs reasonably moist soil, stands more shade.

TULIPS. For grouping in perennial border. Alone in beds or with such plants as forget-me-nots, English daisies, pansies, and primroses. For cutting. Various types, including the short-stemmed single earlies and double earlies, cottage, breeders, lily-flowering, rem-

LIFE CYCLE OF A BULB

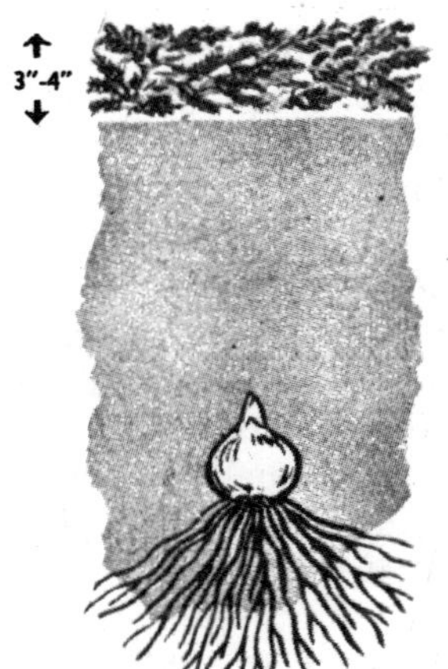

If you slice a bulb in half, you can see through a magnifying glass that it has a complete plant in embryo—or else it won't bloom. Planted at the right time and depth the bulb develops a mass of roots. A winter covering of mulch of 3-4 inches helps bulbs to grow. In the spring the stem pushes upward through the ground covering. At this time remove the winter protection of mulch little by little.

brandts and darwins, which bloom later and have longer stems. Almost every color except real blue. Plant in early November. Protect where winters are severe by mulching after ground has frozen. After foliage dies, lift and store in cool, dry, airy, shady place until fall, or leave undisturbed and plant shallow-rooted annuals, such as portulaca or sweet alyssum, over them. Every third year lift, grade, and plant in new ground. Don't plant tulips in ground from which tulips have been taken for three years. Full sun.

NARCISSI (including Daffodils). For naturalizing in grass, open woodlands, and among shrubbery. For grouping in the perennial border. For cut flowers. Less well adapted than tulips or hyacinths for solid beds, but can be so used. Many types. White, through all shades of yellow and orange; some are nearly pink. Many are highly fragrant. Best to leave them in ground all summer. Lift, grade, and immediately replant in July every third to fifth year. Plant new bulbs as early as they can be obtained (usually in September or in early October). Fertilize established plantings each year in early spring. Prefer light shade.

SPANISH, DUTCH AND ENGLISH IRISES. For grouping in perennial borders. In beds and borders alone or with other flowers. For cutting. All colors except red and pink. Lift and store like tulips each year. Not extremely hardy. In the north plant in a warm sheltered place (close to a south-facing wall, for example) and cover through the winter with a six- or eight-inch layer of leaves or salt hay. Full sun.

Tender Bulbs for Summer Bloom. These bulbs bloom outdoors in summer or fall and are usually stored indoors during the winter. Their tenderness varies. Unless you garden in a decidedly favorable climate, do not set these in the open garden until the weather is settled and fairly warm. Lift them at the first killing frost.

HARDY BULBS TO PLANT IN THE FALL

Ground Level	Tulips	Narcissi and Daffodils and Summer Snowflake	Hyacinths	Crocuses	Grape-Hyacinths, Squills, Snowdrops, Glory-of-the-Snow, Winter-Aconite	Spanish, Dutch, and English Irises	Spanish and English Bluebells	Camassia
1"								
2"								
3"								
4"								
5"								
6"								
7"								
8"								
9"								
Distance Apart	6"	7"-8"	7"-8"	3"-4"	2"-3"	4"-5"	3"-4"	5"-6"

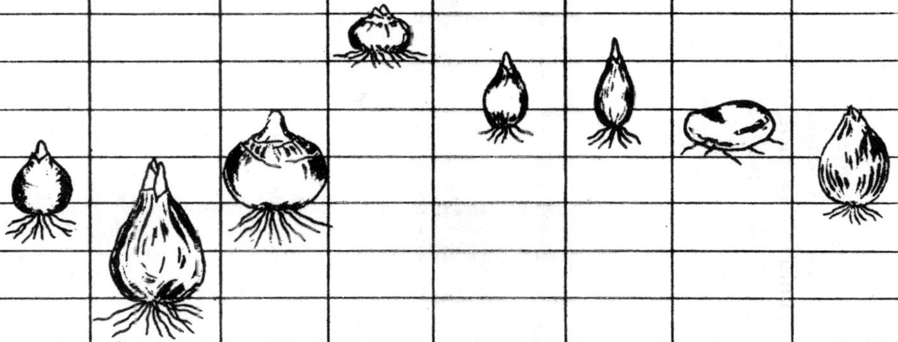

Showing depth below surface tip of bulb should be and distances between bulbs.

ACIDANTHERA. For cutting and garden decoration. 2-2½ feet. Flowers white, marked purple, in late summer. Fragrant. Needs long season of growth. Not suitable for outdoor garden where fall frosts come early. Plant 3 inches deep, 3-4 inches apart. Culture and storage as for gladiolus. In mild climates leave in ground over winter.

AMARCRINUM. For cutting and garden decoration. 3 feet. Flowers pink, fragrant, in late fall. Set 18 inches apart in light, rich well-drained soil. Position: sunny. Lift after first frost; leave soil on the roots. Store in light cool cellar or deep, well-protected frame.

CALADIUM, FANCY-LEAVED. For "tropical" effects. 1½-2 feet. Splendidly colored leaves. Plant tubers or started pot plants 12-15 inches apart after the ground is really warm. Requires rich soil containing humus, shade, plenty of moisture, and shelter from sweeping winds. After the first touch of frost, lift and handle like begonias. Store in 50 to 60 degree temperature.

CANNA. For beds and borders. 2-6 feet. Flowers cream, yellow, orange, red. Start root divisions indoors 12 weeks before planting-out time if it is to be potted, 4-5 weeks before if it is to be set in garden from flats. Plant with "eye" or growing bud 2 inches or less below the surface. Set plants 18 inches apart. After first frost lift, cut stems back to a length of 6 inches. Leave soil dry and store in single layer packed with sand or dry soil in 40-50 degree temperature.

ELEPHANTS EAR (*Colocasia*). For "tropical effects." 6 to 8 feet. Large, handsome leaves. Separate and start tubers in pots indoors 8-10 weeks before setting them in the garden. Don't plant in the open until the soil is warm and the weather is settled. Choose sheltered, partly shaded locations. Provide very rich, moist soil. Store in winter like cannas.

PLANTING LILY BULBS

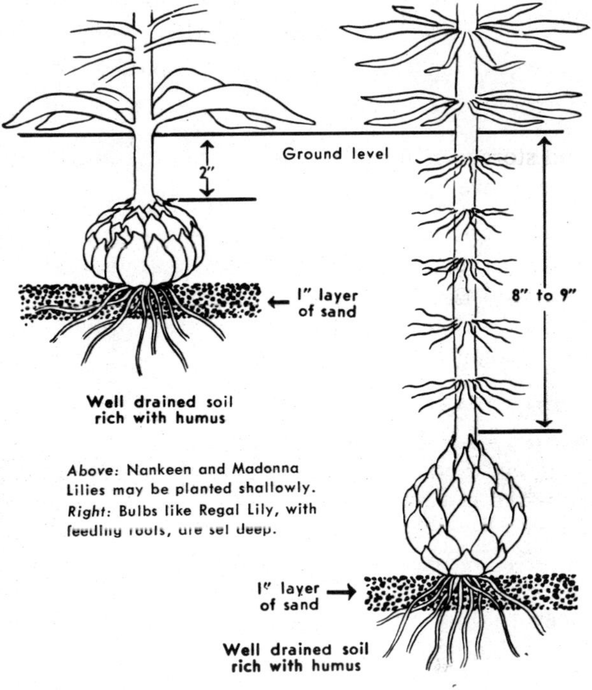

Ground level

2"

1" layer of sand

Well drained soil rich with humus

Above: Nankeen and Madonna Lilies may be planted shallowly. *Right:* Bulbs like Regal Lily, with feeding roots, are set deep.

8" to 9"

1" layer of sand

Well drained soil rich with humus

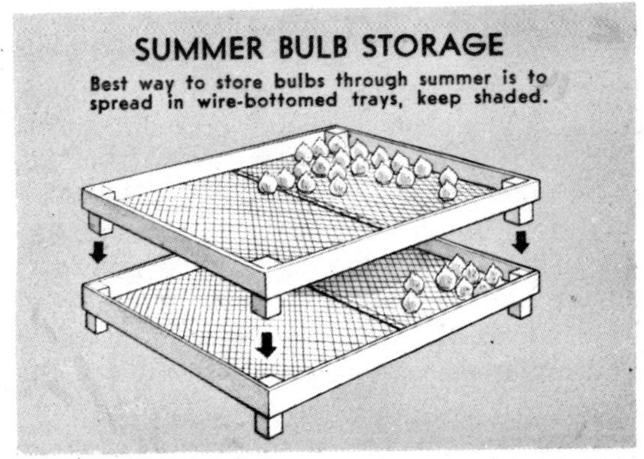

SUMMER BULB STORAGE

Best way to store bulbs through summer is to spread in wire-bottomed trays, keep shaded.

MONTBRETIA. For cutting and garden decoration. 2½ to 3½ feet. Flowers yellow, orange or red. Treat like gladiolus. Plant 3-4 inches deep, 4-5 inches apart.

OXALIS BOWIEANA. For beds and borders. 6-9 inches. Flower is pink; in late summer and fall. Treat like gladiolus. Plant 2-3 inches deep, 3-4 inches apart.

PERUVIAN DAFFODIL (*Ismene*). For garden decoration and cutting. 2 feet. Flowers white or pale yellow, fragrant. Plant 8-10 inches apart in sunny place in well-drained, fertile soil. Cover bulbs with three times their own depth of soil. Store in winter in 60-degree temperature.

SUMMER HYACINTH (*Galtonia*). For beds and borders. 3-5 feet. Flowers cream. Same culture as gladiolus. South of Philadelphia may be left in ground all winter.

TIGER FLOWER. (*Tigridia*). For beds and borders. 1-2 feet. Flowers white, tawny yellow, pink, red, variously spotted and blotched. Plant 5-6 inches apart. Cover bulbs to a depth of 3 inches. Culture as for gladiolus. Store, with foliage still attached, in 55-60 degree temperature. Need warm, sheltered situation.

TUBEROUS BEGONIA. For beds and borders. 1 to 1½ feet. Flowers white, cream, yellow, pink, and red. Start indoors 6-8 weeks before time to transfer plants outdoors, after the ground is warm and the weather is settled. Tubers planted one inch deep directly outdoors when soil is warm bloom later. Space 10 to 12 inches apart. Tuberous begonias need soil rich with humus, shade from strong sun and shelter from strong winds. Keep soil always fairly moist. Lift at first light touch of frost. Do not remove stems or foliage, keep earth on, and place in warm, light place for two or three weeks to encourage tops to dry, then clean off tubers and store packed in peat moss in temperature of 50-55 degrees.

TUBEROSE. For cut flowers and garden decoration. 2-3 feet. Flowers white, fragrant. Plant strong bulbs in rich soil in warm, sunny location when the weather is settled. Set 5-6 inches apart and cover to a depth of 3 inches. A long growing season is needed. In North it may be started indoors in pots. Remove all small offsets from blooming size bulbs before planting. Do not remove foliage at lifting time. Treat like tuberous begonias but store dry with soil attached to their roots in 60-degree temperature throughout the winter.

Some Unusual Bulbs

ATAMASCO OR FAIRY LILY (*Zephyranthes*). For garden decoration. 6-12 inches. White or pink. Plant in the spring, 2-3 inches deep, about 2 inches apart. Full sun. Warm, well-drained soil. *Zephyranthes candida* is hardy in New York. Others are more tender.

AUTUMN CROCUS (*Colchicum*). For garden decoration. 6-9 inches. Flowers are white or pink, in the summer or fall. Large, coarse leaves appear in the spring and die by summer. Plant where dying foliage will not be unsightly. Likes good soil and good drainage. Plant in August-September with tops of bulbs 2-3 inches below the surface. Space 4-6 inches apart.

BELLADONNA LILY (*Amaryllis belladonna*). For garden decoration and cutting. Flower is white or pink. Plant in July-August, 8 to 9 inches deep in warm, fertile, well-drained soil. Leaves appear after flowering. Not reliably hardy north of Washington, D. C.

CRINUM. For garden decoration and cutting. Here belong the "milk-and-wine lilies" of the South. All need full sun, rich soil and plenty of water when actively growing. *Crinum powelli,* the hardiest, lives outdoors in sheltered positions in New York. Plant in spring, 12 inches apart with tips of bulbs just beneath the surface.

FLOWERING ONION (*Allium*). For garden decoration. Many very different kinds. Among the best are *moly* (yellow), *neapolitanum* (white) and *albopilosum* (blue-gray). All need well-drained soil, and most require full sun. *Moly* stands shade.

HARDY AMARYLLIS (*Lycoris*). For garden decoration and cutting. 2-3 feet. Flowers lavender lilac in August. Plant in July. Leaves appear in spring, die down before flowers appear. Full sun. Fertile, well-drained soil.

ORNITHOGALUM. For garden decoration and cut flowers. White, gray or yellow. For garden decoration. Several distinct kinds. *Nutans* is one of the hardiest; *arabicum* is one of the best but it is hardy in fairly mild climates only. Plant 4 inches deep in rich soil, in sun or light shade.

SPRING STAR-FLOWER (*Triteleia* or *Brodiaea uniflora*). For garden decoration. 3 inches. Pale blue. Plant in light, well-drained soil, in a sunny position. Hardy in sheltered locations in New York.

STERNBERGIA. For garden decoration. Resembles bright yellow crocus. 3-4 inches. Give sunny sheltered position and well-drained soil. Plant in the spring.

These Real Lilies Are Easy

Only plants that bear the botanical name *Lilium* are true lilies. Others, such as day lilies, plantain lilies, water lilies, and lilies-of-the-valley, are not. Some lilies are very difficult to grow, others thrive without trouble. Among the easiest are the many selected hybrid kinds now offered in dealers' catalogs and there described, and the following species.

LILIUM CANDIDUM (*Madonna lily*). Blooms in July. White. Not stem-rooting.

LILIUM ELEGANS. Blooms in July. Red. Stem-rooting.

LILIUM HANSONI (*Hanson's lily*). Blooms in June and July. Yellow. Stem-rooting.

LILIUM HENRYI (*Henry's lily*). Blooms in August and September. Yellow-orange. Stem-rooting.

LILIUM PARDALINUM. Blooms in July. Orange. Stem-rooting.

LILIUM PUMILUM. Blooms in June and July. Red. Stem-rooting.

LILIUM REGALE (*Regal lily*). Blooms in July. White. Stem-rooting.

LILIUM SPECIOSUM. Blooms in August and September. White or pink. Stem-rooting.

LILIUM TESTACEUM (*Nankeen lily*). Blooms in July. Apricot. Not stem-rooting.

LILIUM TRIGRINUM (*Tiger lily*). Blooms in August. Orange. Stem-rooting.

LILIUM UMBELLATUM. Blooms in July and August. Yellow-orange. Stem-rooting.

Buy lily bulbs that are disease-free, plump, fresh, and with live roots. Plant in fall (Madonna lily in August) or early spring in well-drained soil that contains plenty of humus. Lilies appreciate light shade from hot sun. In summer, mulch with peat moss or leaf mold; in winter, with partly rotted leaves or salt hay.

Rock Gardens

✣✣

Gardening offers nothing finer than a well planned, skillfully planted rock garden, nothing more atrocious than a bad one. The peanut-brittle type of bank, border, or bed studded with regularly placed rocks that stand more or less on end represents an all-time low in poor landscaping. Don't inflict it on your friends and neighbors. Justify your rock garden either on the grounds that your land is rocky or sloping and hence is a "natural" for this type of development, or on the basis that you wish to grow a variety of plants not easily accommodated in ordinary beds and borders. Rock gardens in level, rockless parts of the country are not out of place if well done, and if they serve this latter purpose.

Your rock garden may be (1) entirely natural; (2) completely artificial, or (3) a mixture of both. Natural outcrops can often be planted attractively with no preparation other than clearing away unwanted trees, brush, and coarse herbage, and deepening and filling with porous, fertile soil whatever pockets and crevices exist in and between the rocks.

Judicious removal of soil from around an outcrop will sometimes reveal beautiful rock previously buried. By baring portions you may be able to add to the extent and impressiveness of your garden.

Often natural rockwork can be improved by construct-

A beautiful rock garden is an artful deception—it looks "natural" but is the product of careful work.

ing additional ledges and outcrops near it. Let such additions be of native stone arranged to blend perfectly with the natural feature. When assembling stone for a constructed rock garden, choose pieces with well-weathered surfaces, of a character and coloring that suggest great age. Avoid newly quarried rocks, round, hard boulders and thin, flat slabs. These are difficult to arrange convincingly.

Best of all are waterworn limestone, soft sandstone, and rocks of similar porous character. Tufa is light and easy to handle, but except in desert regions it usually looks a little out of place. In naturally rocky regions it is generally best to employ the type of rock natural to the locality.

Before you begin construction have in mind a clear idea of the feature you are trying to create. You need not copy any specific piece of natural rockwork, but if your garden is of the naturalistic type it should appear as if it could have been created by Nature. Don't let it look as if a couple of truckloads of rocks had been dumped on the ground and filled over with soil.

A mistake commonly made is to have the rocks all about the same size. Don't do this. It gives the garden a mechanical appearance. Even a few big rocks skillfully located give character. Use streamers, ledges and minor outcrops of lesser rocks to complete the picture. Don't dot rocks over the entire area. Flats, gentle slopes and flower-decked meadows may occupy the spaces between the rocky outcrops. You may have read rules to the effect that one-third, one-half, or two-thirds of each rock should be beneath the soil surface. Nonsense. The important thing is that the groupings look as if they are part of outcropping bed rock and as if they were connected one to the other underground. If you succeed it does not matter what proportion of each individual rock is buried. A feeling of stability is essential. Loose pieces on or at the surface should be used only as they might occur in rocky country, as if broken from the parent bed rock.

Be very careful to keep the parallel strata lines that show on the faces of most rocks running at about the same angle and in the same direction throughout the garden. If tilted

RIGHT

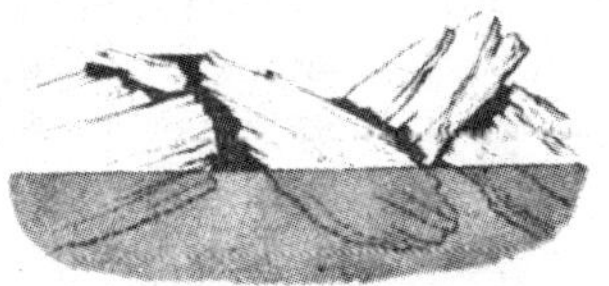

When placing rocks on the surface arrange them so that strata lines run in the same direction, as shown at left—not at random, as shown in arrangement at right.

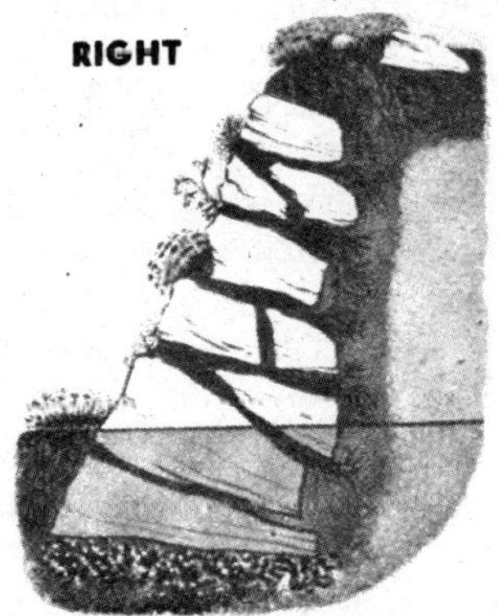

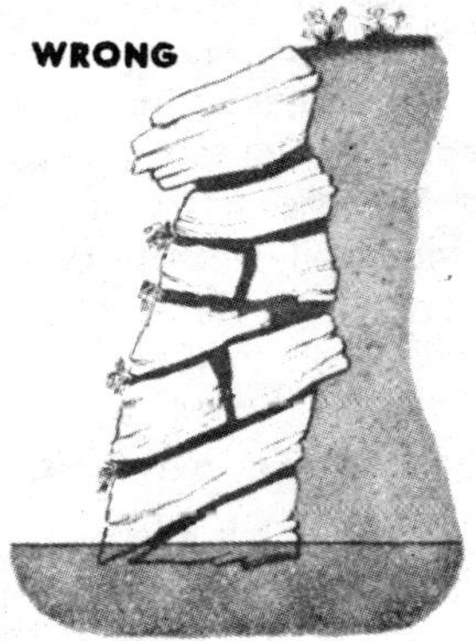

Rocks imbedded in an incline should not overhang those below them. Correct structure is shown at left; structure at right is not satisfactory for plant.

slightly from the horizontal, these usually give the most satisfactory effect. Begin building the rock garden at the lowest part and work upward and backwards. Expose the weathered face of the rocks to view and, wherever it can be done without losing effectiveness, tilt the rocks so their top surfaces carry water back to the roots. Pack the soil firmly around each rock; don't leave air pockets. Arrange simple stepping-stone or other appropriate paths so that reasonable access to the plants is possible.

Water in the form of a cascade, stream or pool adds tremendously to the delight of a rock garden. It gives life to the picture and attracts birds. It also gives logical reason for growing a few bog plants near the margins of the water. Fit the water feature compatibly into the design. See that a pool occupies a natural looking hollow and that cascades do not spout from the tops of rocks but originate part way down a slope.

Naturalistic rock gardens fit well into natural landscapes. It is also possible to have delightful formalized rock gardens, banks, or terraces obviously constructed, not intended to imitate nature, and paved paths with tiny plants in the crevices. Tastefully planted, dry walls (walls in which soil substitutes for cement) fit well into developments of this kind.

The soil must drain freely. See that it is gritty and porous. If heavy, the addition of one-third part by bulk of coarse sand or coal cinders is helpful. Use plenty of humus, leaf mold or peat moss, and some bone meal. A soil of this character suits most plants; modify it locally to meet the requirements of highly specialized kinds if this seems desirable. Try to have a foot or more of prepared soil where-ever you plant. Rock plants root deeply. Spring or early fall are the best planting seasons. Set most of the plants out in natural-looking drifts and groups rather than singly or evenly spaced in regular shaped patches. Never let the plants dry out. Spread their roots carefully at planting time and firm the soil well about them. Immediately after planting, water thoroughly.

Rockfoils.

Grape hyacinths.

Crocus speciosus.

Alpine bellflowers.

Sun roses.

Silene alpestris.

Oxalis bowieana.

Campanula carpatica.

One cannot generalize about the needs of rock plants. There are thousands of different kinds from which a selection can be made for almost any situation. Study dealers' lists carefully. Try to choose wisely. Give consideration to the known requirements of particular plants. Let this consideration take priority over color arrangement or other purely aesthetic matters.

Once constructed, a rock garden does not call for much hard work. Its upkeep is relatively easy. In spring give attention to uncovering, to pushing back plants that have heaved, and to dividing and re-setting.

A Selection of Rock Garden Plants For Sun

Achillea serbica
Achillea tomentosa
Adonis amurensis
Aethionema grandiflorum
Aethionema pulchellum
Aethionema Warley Hybrid
Alyssum montanum
Alyssum saxatile
Alyssum saxatile luteum
Androsace lanuginosa
Androsace sarmentosa
Anthemis montana
Aquilegia flabellata nana
Arabis albida
Arabis procurrens
Arenaria montana
Armeria caespitosa
Bellium minutum
Campanula cochlearifolia
Campanula garganica
Campanula portenschlagiana
Campanula poscharskyana
Ceratostigma plumbaginoides
Dianthus alpinus
Dianthus arenarius
Dianthus caesius
Dianthus superbus
Erinus alpinus
Geranium cinereum
Geranium lancastriense
Gypsophila cerastiodes
Gypsophila fratensis
Gypsophila repens
Helianthemums (many kinds)
Iris cristata
Iris pumila
Linaria aequitriloba
Linaria pilosa
Linum alpinum
Linum salsoloides
Lychnis alpina
Mazus reptans
Papaver alpinum
Phlox subulata (many kinds)
Polemonium reptans
Potentilla verna nana
Saponaria ocymoides
Saxifraga macnabiana
Sedum (many kinds)
Sempervivums (many kinds)
Silene alpestris
Silene maritima
Thymes (many kinds)
Tunica saxifraga
Valeriana supina
Veronica armena
Veronica filifolia
Veronica pectinata
Veronica repens
Veronica rupestris

Rock Plants For Shade

Aquilegia canadensis
Arenaria balearica
Asperula odorata
Companula rotundifolia
Chrysogonum virginianum
Corydalis lutea
Cotula squalida
Dicentra exima
Epimedium (many kinds)
Ferns (many kinds)
Hepaticas (many kinds)
Houstonia coerulea
Mertensia virginica
Myosotis palustris semperflorens
Myosotis sylvatica
Nierembergia rivularis
Phlox divaricata
Podophyllum peltatum
Polygonatum biflorum
Primula denticulata
Primula japonica
Primula sieboldii
Primula veris
Primula vulgaris
Primula vulgaris coerulea
Pulmonaria angustifolia
Sanguinaria canadensis
Sedum ternatum
Silene pennsylvanica
Silene virginica
Thalictrum kiusianum
Thalictrum minus
Vancouveria hexandra
Violas (many kinds)

Bulbs For The Rock Garden

For Sun

Allium cyaneum
(and other dwarf kinds)
"Botanical" tulips
Crocus species
Dwarf Narcissi
Glories-of-the-snow
Grape hyacinths
Snowdrops
Squills

For Shade

Allium moly
Anemones (many kinds)
Bellwort
Bloodroot
Dutchman's Breeches
Jack-in-the-Pulpit
May-apple
Rue Anemone
Spring beauties
Squirrel Corn
Trilliums
Trout lilies

Dwarf Evergreens (All except the yews, rhododendrons, and hemlocks need full sun.)

Alberta spruce
Creeping junipers
Dwarf arbovitaes
Dwarf firs
Dwarf hemlocks
Dwarf mugho pine
Dwarf yews
Brooms (many kinds)
Dwarf barberries
Dwarf rhododendrons
Heaths and heathers
Sand-myrtle
Santolina
Spike-heath

The Garden Pool

***

Nowhere can water lilies be grown to greater perfection than in the U. S. For this reason and because water is such an interesting landscape element, have a garden pool if you can. Its value as a mirror, the feeling of coolness and tranquility it gives, and the opportunity it provides to accommodate goldfish and such are appealing.

Water plants are easy to grow, need no cultivation, staking, tying or watering. Weeding is almost non-existent and they are free from diseases and insects.

If you have a natural pond or if one can be made by damming a stream you are fortunate. Otherwise you must construct a pool. Usually this will be of concrete, although a clay-bottomed pool may do. A miniature pool can be made of a sawed-off tub sunk into the ground.

Two basic problems must be met: (1) Assure yourself of a supply of water. (2) Make certain the pool can be drained.

Still water suits aquatics best. But water is needed and occasionally it must be replenished and changed.

The size of the pool should be in scale with the surrounding landscape.

Pools may be formal, geometrical using neat curbs defining them, or they may be informal and naturalistic. In formal surroundings the former is better; in naturalistic surroundings the latter is usually preferred.

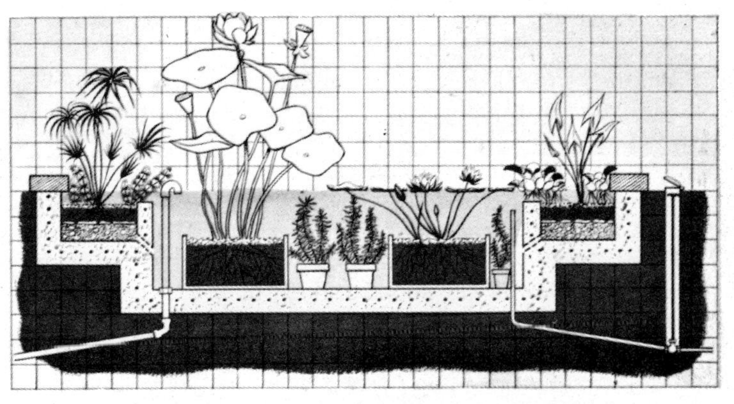

Section of a typical garden pool of reinforced concrete. Note shelves for shallow plants. One square equals half-foot. Close-up is of the ever-popular water lily.

A formal pool edged with stone. Water lilies, aquatic irises, and other water-loving plants flourish here.

Before you make a decision outline your proposed pool on the ground, using stakes linked together with strings or garden hose.

Small pools can be filled conveniently by the garden hose. For larger ones it is better to pipe water to them. Make sure

A drain that also serves as an overflow is ideal. It may lead to sewer, ditch, stream, dry well, or to some place below the level of the pool bottom where the water may seep away or evaporate.

out of the water to a height of two or three feet, the

All pipes that lead into or away from the pool should be in position before concrete is poured.

Small pools can be emptied by siphoning the water away through a hose. Fill it with water. Do not let air enter. Place one end in the pool, the other at a lower level. Open the lower end.

that (1) the supply lines are buried well below frost level or (2) provision is made to drain them in winter. The first is safer. Do not install fountains that cause much inflow.

A depth of two feet is desirable for pools that are to contain water lilies in tubs; twenty inches is a minimum. If planted in soil placed on the bottom of the pool, fifteen inches is enough. Roots should be eight to twelve inches under water.

Water Lilies. Hardy water lilies may be left out all winter if they are under so much water that their tubers do not freeze or if, after the pool is drained, they are protected from freezing by a thick layer of leaves placed over them. They may be taken indoors and buried in moist sand where a 40 to 50 degree temperature is maintained. Tropical water lilies are not winter-hardy except in the warmest areas; ordinarily they must be replaced yearly.

Water lilies are gross feeders. They like a rich, loamy soil. Good garden soil mixed with half its bulk of rotted cow-manure and a pint of bone meal and a pint of dried blood or tankage added to each bushel is ideal. If you cannot get rotted cow manure, use dried sheep manure, with one part to ten parts soil.

Plant hardy water lilies in spring just before the trees open their buds; tropical water lilies, only when the weather is warm and settled. Do not plant tropicals unless the water has been warmed.

Other Aquatics

THE LOTUSES. Looking like great tropical lilies but with huge shield-like leaves and large flowers that rise out of the water to a height of two or three feet, the lotuses are grand plants for the garden pool. They require the same treatment as hardy water lilies. The American lotus has yellow flowers, the Egyptian, pink, the Japanese, white, the Chinese, red, and Shiroman, white. All have decorative seed pods.

SHALLOW WATER PLANTS. For planting in shallow water—where the soil is covered to a depth of from one to three inches make a selection from the following: Arrowhead, Floatingheart, Flowering rush, Marsh Marigold, Pickerel rush, Sweet Flag, Wild Calla, Water snowflake, Parrot feather, Water poppy, Water clover, and Velvet Leaf. All of these grow well in any good garden soil. The first seven are hardy outdoors. The other five should be wintered indoors in a pool or aquarium in the North.

FLOATING PLANTS. You will like for your pool some of the following plants which float freely on the surface and need not be planted in soil. In the North all of these should be taken indoors during the winter. Azolla, water fern, Water lettuce, and Water hyacinth.

SUBMERGED PLANTS. These submerged plants oxygenate the water, keep it pure, and improve it for fish: Anacharis, Cabomba, Coon tail, Milfoil, Needle leaf Ludwigia, and Tape Grass. Plant them in soil in containers, in the bottom of the pool, or in shallow water.

BOG PLANTS. Plants that naturally grow in bogs are appropriate for planting at the margins of pools. Among the most suitable are: Yellow flag iris, Marsh iris, Water forget-me-not, Cardinal flower, Bog bean, and Narrow leaved cat-tail, all of which are hardy, as well as such tender plants as Papyrus, Taro, Crinum lily, Ginger lily, Thalia, and Umbrella palm.

Your Own Vegetable Garden

The production of crops to eat has been of primary concern since man ceased to depend upon wild vegetation and hunting as a means of sustenance. It is still basic to his existence.

Because cultivating a vegetable garden gives opportunity to participate in food production it satisfies a fundamental urge latent in every normal individual.

Those who say "I can buy vegetables cheaper" simply miss the point, for the values one gets from cultivating a kitchen garden are not expressable in terms of money. Furthermore they are rarely right. For with properly directed effort you can, in any reasonable garden soil and situation, grow a variety of vegetables far cheaper than you can buy them. Always supposing of course, that you do not charge for your own labor. Modern freezing methods make it easy to store excess. There need be no waste.

The requirements for a successful vegetable plot are: a fairly good soil or one that can be made so, a reasonably level, sunny situation, a water supply, and know-how with the ability to apply it.

A vegetable garden must be well drained. If the water table is so high that the soil is saturated to within a foot or so of the surface, you face serious difficulties.

Apply yourself diligently then to conditioning and improving the soil during the time when it is free of crops.

Dig, manure fertilize, and lime it as occasion demands, and as opportunity occurs.

Look after your soil at other times, too. Don't walk upon it more than is absolutely necessary when it is wet, especially if it is at all heavy. To do so compacts it and destroys its texture.

Size. It is a mistake to attempt too large a garden. A plot fifty by forty feet is about the maximum that an able-bodied person can care for adequately in his spare time. This will require an average of thirty hours of labor a month through the season.

Gardens worked with hand tools can be much more closely cropped than is possible where machine tools are used. Under such intensive cultivation the weight of crops obtained per unit area is surprisingly large.

Plan. Plan your garden on paper. Let the plan be simple. Elaborate systems of paths, cute little edgings and the like are out of place in this type of development. Let functionalism prevail. After all, nothing looks better in a vegetable garden than straight rows of healthy vegetables. They are beautiful in themselves. This does not mean that you should not set aside a corner for a few flowers. Just don't mess up the whole area with them.

Your first year's plan will not work out entirely right. Keep careful records and notes of the garden and amend the plan the following year. Do this annually.

Among the chief matters of concern in planning are rotations (do not plant the same kind of crops in the same place each year), successions (how to space sowings so that a continuous supply of vegetables results and what to plant to follow crops harvested early), amounts (the beginner almost always plants too much of some crops and too little of others), and grouping (arranging the crops so that definite areas of the garden become vacant at one time and can be conditioned and replanted more or less together, and so that crops that occupy the ground through almost the entire season such as pole-beans, corn, tomatoes, eggplants, and

	Sow, and Thin Out Seedlings if Necessary	Sow, and Transplant Seedlings	Sow Early Indoors or in Frame	Sow Early Outdoors	Sow After Ground is Warm and Weather is Settled	Make Successional Sowings	Approximate Number of Days From Sowing to Harvesting	Distance Apart Between Rows. In Inches	Distance in Inches Between Plants or Between Hills in Rows	Depth to Sow in Inches	Amount of Seed Per 100 Feet in Ounces	Comments
Beans, Dwarf or Bush					✓	✓	45 55	24	3	1	8	Do not work among when wet.
Beans, Pole					✓		65	48	36	1	4	Do not work among when wet. Plant in hills.
Beans, Bush Lima					✓		75	27	3	1	10	Tender, don't plant too early.
Beans, Pole Lima					✓		85	48	36	1	8	Plant in hills. Tender, don't plant too early.
Beets				✓		✓	55–70	12–14	3	3/4	1	Will not thrive if soil is acid. Sow thinly, each "seed" is really several seeds stuck together and produces several plants.
Broccoli		✓	✓	✓		✓	60–100	36	20	1/2	1/4	Provides picking over long periods.
Brussels Sprouts		✓			✓		90–120	36	20	1/2	1/4	Select sowing date so that crop matures after killing frost.
Cabbage, Early and Mid-Season		✓	✓			✓	80–90	24	15–20	1/2	1/4	Do not plant too many of any one kind. All plants of a variety mature together.
Cabbage, Late		✓		✓	✓		100–120	30–36	20–24	1/2	1/4	Select sowing date so crop matures at end of summer.

Carrots	√			√		√	65–80	12	2–3	1/2	1/4	Thrive only in well worked, mellow soils free of clods and roughage.
Cauliflower		√	√	√	√	√	80–110	24–30	18–24	1/2	1/4	A difficult crop to grow except where cool summers prevail.
Celery		√	√			√	110–140	24	6	1/16	1 pkt.	Needs rich soil and abundant moisture.
Celeriac	√	√			√		120	18	6	1/4	1 pkt.	Easier to grow than celery, requires moist soil.
Chinese Cabbage	√	√				√	80–100	15–18	8–10	1/2	1/4	In north is best grown as fall crop; in south as a winter crop. Needs cool weather.
Collards	√		√	√		√	65–70	24–30	15–18	1/2	1/4	Very hardy and easy to grow. Stand hot weather well.
Corn	√				√	√	65–100	30–36	9–12	1	4	Better in rows than in hills.
Cucumber	√		√		√		60–72	48	18	1	1/2	Will not thrive if soil is acid. Needs plenty of moisture.
Eggplant		√	√				125–135	30–36	24	1/2	1 pkt.	Heavy feeder, needs rich, moist ground.
Endive	√	√	√	√		√	45	18	9–12	1/2	1/4	Sow also in late summer for fall use.
Florence Fennell	√					√	85	18	4	1/2	1/4	Draw soil up about bases of plants when they are about as big as eggs.
Kale		√			√		50–65	20–24	12	1/2	1 pkt.	Very hardy. Light fall frost improves its flavor.
Kohlrabi	√			√		√	65	15	3–4	1/2	1/4	If not grown quickly the roots are tough and woody.
Leeks		√	√	√			130	18–24	4–6	1/3	1/4	Plant in trenches or deep drills so that plants can be "earthed up" with soil to blanch them. Do not earth up early in season or plants may rot.

	Sow, and Thin Out Seedlings if Necessary	Sow, and Transplant Seedlings	Sow Early Indoors or in Frame	Sow Early Outdoors	Sow After Ground is Warm and Weather is Settled	Make Successional Sowings	Approximate Number of Days From Sowing to Harvesting	Distance Apart Between Rows. In Inches	Distance in Inches Between Plants or Between Hills in Rows	Depth to Sow in Inches	Amount of Seed Per 100 Feet in Ounces	Comments
Lettuce, Head	✓	✓	✓	✓	✓	✓	50	15	9–12	1/4	1 pkt.	Make frequent sowings to insure succession. Select special varieties for hot weather sowing.
Lettuce, Leaf	✓		✓	✓	✓	✓	45	15	3–6	1/4	1 pkt.	Make frequent sowings to insure succession. Select special varieties for hot weather sowing.
Muskmelon or Cantaloupe	✓				✓		75–80	60	48	1/2	1/2	Sow in hills, 8 to 10 seeds to each. Thin to 3 or 4.
Okra	✓				✓		65–70	30–36	15–20	1/2	1/2	Pick pods while they are young and tender and use them promptly.
Onions	✓		✓	✓		✓	120	12–15	2–4	1/2	1/4	Onions raised from seeds keep better through the winter than those raised from sets. Be sure that onions to be stored ripen thoroughly before storing.
Parsley	✓			✓			90–95	15	4–6	1/3	1/4	Likes firm soil. Apply light dressings of fertilizer through growing season.
Parsnip	✓			✓			120	18	3–4	1/2	1/2	Are improved by frost, do not dig too early.
Peas	✓			✓		✓	50–60	36–60	1	1	16	Distinctly a cool weather crop. Sow as early as possible. Varieties that grow more than 2½ feet tall need supporting with brush wood or chicken wire. Sowings made late in summer yield fall crops.

Peppers		√	√				115	30–36	18–20	1/2	1 pkt.	Excessive amounts of nitrogen in the soil may prevent the flowers from setting fruits.
Pumpkins	√				√		60–75	60	60	1	1/2	Sow in hills, 6 or 8 seeds to each, later thin the plants out 3 to a hill.
Radishes	√			√		√	30–35	12	1–2	1/2	1/2	Sow every two or three weeks for succession. Thrive best in cool weather.
Rutabaga	√						90	18	6–10	1/4	1/4	Sow so that crop reaches maturity after fall frost. Avoid sowing too early.
Soy Beans	√				√	√	90–120	24–36	3–4	1	8–16	Well suited for warmer parts of the country.
Spinach	√			√		√	50–60	12–14	3–4	1/2	1/2	Sow every two weeks for succession. Succeeds best in cool weather.
Spinach, New Zealand	√				√		35–45	12–18	12–18	1	1	Produces all summer if main shoot is not picked.
Squash	√				√		55–95	48	48	3/4	1/2	Needs rich, warm, well drained soil. Sow in hills, 6 or 8 seeds to each; later thin plants to 3 to a hill.
Swiss Chard	√			√			50	18–20	6	1/2	1	Stands summer heat well. Apply light applications of fertilizer during the growing season. Pick leaves that are young.
Tomato		√	√				115	36–48	30–48	1/4	1 pkt.	Best for garden purposes when staked and trained to one or two stems, or grown on trellis and pruned.
Turnip	√			√		√	60–70	14–16	3–4	1/2	1/2	Distinctly a cool weather crop. Sow in late summer for fall crops.
Watermelon	√				√		85–90	96	96	1/2	1/2	Plant wilt-resisting kinds only. Plant in hills.
Witloof Chicory	√				√		95	24	3	1/2	1	After freezing "force" roots indoors, for winter vegetable or salad.

that are not dry. Set plants 8 by 8 feet apart. Cultivate frequently but shallowly or mulch with peat moss. Plant two compatible varieties together to ensure fruit. Use acid fertilizer only. Prune out old, unproductive wood.

CHERRY, SWEET. Prefer light soils. Obtain trees on Mazzard roots. Set 25 to 30 feet apart. Does not like hot summers. Susceptible to severe winter cold. Keep ground cultivated or mulched. Little fertilizing needed. Mature trees need no pruning other than removal of dead, injured, and occasionally unwanted branches. Three spray applications required.

CHERRY, SOUR, AND DUKE. Any good soil. Stand much more cold and heat than sweet cherry, and in most places are easier to grow, particularly the sours. Obtain trees on Mazzard roots. Set sours 18 feet, dukes 22 feet apart. General care same as for sweet cherries.

CURRANTS, RED, AND WHITE. Rich, heavy, fairly moist soil is best. Likes cool climate. Fertilize freely. Mulch. Set one- or two-year-old plants 4 to 5 feet apart in rows 6 feet apart. Prune out all branches when they become three or four years old. Each year allow two or three of the strongest new shoots to mature. Remove others early. Four or five spray applications needed.

FIG. Moist heavy loams, well limed, are best. Plant 10 to 30 feet apart—the greater distance in mild climates. Prune to encourage development of many new shoots each year. Mulch or cultivate shallowly. Fertilize freely. In North protect trees in winter by wrapping them in heavy burlap, or some similar material, and by applying a heavy mulch over their roots.

GOOSEBERRY. Cultivate as advised for currants. Appreciates very light shade.

GRAPE. Any ordinary soil well supplied with humus and not excessively rich. Plant one-year vines 8 or 9 feet apart each way. Self-sterile varieties must be interplanted with pollinator varieties to ensure fruit. Train to wires, trellis, or other supports. Cultivate shallowly, or mulch. Fruit is borne on new wood. Prune with this in mind. Six or seven spray applications normally required.

NECTARINE. Cultivation same as for peach.

PEACH. Light, well-drained, warm soil. Sheltered position on fairly high ground, preferably sloping to west or north. Set 18 feet apart each way. Keep ground cultivated or mulched, never in sod. Avoid excessive fertilization. Prune freely to encourage strong young fruiting wood. Thin fruits to 4 or 5 inches apart about four weeks after they set. Most varieties are self-fertile; a few need other varieties nearby as pollinators. Three to five spray applications needed.

PEAR. Prefers heavy, but will grow in any ordinary soil if not extremely dry. Plant in fall or very early spring. Set 20 to 25 feet apart. Pears are subject to fire blight, particularly during their youth. To minimize the possibility of this avoid over-fertilization with nitrogen and do minimum amount of pruning until trees begin to bear. Excessive growth encourages the disease. Growing in sod rather than in mulched or cultivated soil is advisable. Fruits on spurs, prune accordingly. Five or six spray applications needed.

PLUM. European varieties prefer rich heavy soils, Japanese and American varieties like lighter soils. Set trees 15 to 20 feet apart. Cultivate shallowly or mulch. Avoid overstimulation with nitrogen. Don't do more pruning than absolutely necessary. Thin fruits by removing 20 to 50 per cent immediately following the natural June drop. Three spray applications needed.

QUINCE. Soil warm, well drained, deep, moderately fertile. Plant 15 feet apart. Plant only stock propagated by layering. Train as bushes rather than as trees. This permits removal of branches affected with fire blight without total loss. Prune to keep top open with branches well spread out. Cultivate shallowly. Avoid overstimulation with nitrogen.

RASPBERRY. Soil deep, well drained, fairly heavy. Good air drainage is necessary. Avoid low lying frost pockets. Plant disease-free plants in spring. Plant reds and others with suckers 3 feet apart in rows 6 feet apart, blacks and other non-suckering kinds in hills 5 feet apart. Cut to within 6 inches of the ground at planting time. Prune blacks like blackberries. Prune reds, purples, and other suckering kinds by cutting out old canes after fruiting. Thin others to retain three or four to each foot of row. Tie to wires. Two or three spray applications needed in addition to other control measures for particular insects and diseases.

STRAWBERRY. Soil rich, fairly moist, well prepared. Thrives best where cool seasons prevail. Plant self-fertile varieties and on cultivated land only, where sod has not been for two or three years. Plant runners in spring, potted plants in July or August, 2 feet apart in rows 3 feet apart with crowns just level with surface. Allow two runners from each plant (one on each side) to root into row so that plants are finally 8 inches apart. Remove all other runners. Alternatively plant 18 inches apart in rows 2 feet apart and keep all runners off. Mulch 2 or 3 inches deep with salt hay or leaves after ground has frozen. Remove mulch from plants in spring, but leave between rows and under plants. After fruiting, cut foliage close to ground and rake off old mulch material. Fertilize and cultivate shallowly, and rake half an inch of soil over old crowns. Replant every year or second year in new location. Three or four spray applications needed.

Herbs—for Flavor and Fragrance

Herbs grow well in places where most garden plants would not be particularly happy. Nearly all flourish in gravelly or sandy soils too lean to nourish a worthwhile cabbage or to support a respectable delphinium. Almost all need full sun. Many stand drought well.

Not only do herbs thrive, but their products are superior when they develop under these conditions. The fragrant ones smell better, the savory ones taste better than if they are grown on fat, fertile land.

Although the soil for herbs should be sparingly fertile, see that it is prepared deeply. Have the sub-surface drainage sharp except perhaps for mints, sweet flag, sweet cicely, angelica and lovage, which prefer fairly moist root runs. Fertilize freely with bone meal and unleached wood ashes. Apply lime generously. Very few herbs like acid soils.

Choose a sheltered location for your herb garden so that breezes do not easily dissipate the perfumes, and so that such lovers of cozy warmth as rosemary, borage, and southernwood will flourish.

Because people through the ages have used a vast number of different plants for flavor, fragrance, and as cures or supposed cures for their ills, enthusiastic herb gardeners admit a great array into their collections. We shall limit ourselves to the more important.

Perennial Herbs. Notable among herbs that persist from year to year are different kinds of mints and thymes, sage, tarragon, pot marjoram, costmary, horehound, hyssop, chamomile, lavender, southernwood, wormwood, rue, chives, tansy, angelica, garlic, rosemary, balm, horseradish, winter savory and a number of artemisias.

Some (ordinary sage and common thyme for example), are easily raised from seeds, but tarragon, garlic and certain others can not be so propagated. All can be increased vegetatively by division or cuttings. If you intend to raise slow-growing perennials such as lavender, from seeds, sow them indoors eight or ten weeks before the plants you raise can be set outdoors.

Biennial Herbs. Caraway, parsley, and clary are the chief biennial herbs; the kinds that die during their second summer. Raise new crops each year. Sow the seeds of parsley early, but do not plant caraway or clary until June, otherwise they run to poor flower and die the first year.

Annual Herbs. Grow anise, dill, borage, pot marigold, chervil, coriander, cumin, sweet fennel, sweet basil, bush basil, summer savory, sesame, and nasturtium from seeds sown in the open garden in spring. Certain perennials including sage and thyme can be treated as annuals if desired. In practically all cases sowing outdoors early is to be preferred to raising young plants inside and transplanting although you may find this latter advantageous if spring comes very late in your locality. Of most annuals make more than one sowing during spring and early summer so that you will have other plants when the earliest sown are harvested.

Care Of The Garden. The herb garden calls for little hard work, mostly just day to day attention, good housekeeping as it were. Weeding and shallow cultivation, pinching, sheering back, and harvesting as the needs of the plants demand; in addition, the collection of seeds for sowing at once or in the future will keep you busy.

Take Some Indoors. In early fall, well before killing frost, carefully transplant some chives, parsley, basil, chervil, tarragon, balm, and mint to pots. Use a well drained soil and keep the plants in the shade for a week or ten days before you bring them in. During winter keep them in a sunny window in a fairly cool room. They will provide you with useful pickings. Do not bring the mint indoors until frozen.

The Shady Garden

✣✣✣

Gardening in shade is quite different from gardening in sun. Its problems are different; the effects attained are different, and the plants used are mostly different, too.

In heavy or moderate shade, rely mostly upon form, texture, and varying tones of green to create summer pictures—the bright colors of the sunny garden are not available to you. The shady garden in summer is cool and restful rather than gay and brilliant.

In spring it is different. You may then have a variety of colorful flowers.

To garden well in shade you must adjust your plantings to the environment, which is very different from that of the sunny garden. The differences are not those of light intensity alone. Temperature, atmospheric humidity, soil moisture, root competition, and other factors play their parts.

Kinds of Shade. There are different kinds of shade. Under dense evergreens where the ground is darkened the year 'round, little or nothing will grow. Deciduous trees that cast heavy shade in summer may admit of the cultivation beneath them of plants that grow in the spring only.

Trees that carry not-too-dense foliage such as the pin oak and birches, and those that admit plenty of side light

What can be more pleasant and attractive than a shady garden? But you must know its problems.

because their lowest branches are fairly high give opportunity to grow a greater variety beneath them.

That charming shade that results from sunshine filtering through a light overhead canopy makes possible the most lovely of all shady gardens.

Also to be considered are situations that are in full sun for part of each day and are shaded for the remainder. They give ample scope for interesting plantings.

Causes of Shade. Consider, too, the cause of the shade. Buildings, walls, and nonliving fences make no demands upon the soil. Trees, shrubs and hedges do.

It is often this root competition rather than actual shade that may make it just about impossible to grow anything underneath Norway maples and beech trees. Deep rooting trees that cast the same amount of shade as the maples or beeches present much more favorable planting opportunities. Distant trees may cast shade beyond the influence of their roots. This type of shade is favorable.

The Soil. The principles of soil improvement and management discussed in the chapter "Garden Soils" apply to the shady as well as to the sunny garden. Deep preparation, adequate sub-surface drainage, and the desirability of a fairly high humus content are important.

The majority of shade-loving plants appreciate more humus in the soil than is normally provided in the sunny garden. They are woodlanders accustomed to benefiting from an annual leaf fall. The liberal admixture of old, rotted manure, leaf mold, compost and peat moss with the soil helps them tremendously and so do mulches of these or similar materials. Give this your attention. Another advantage of mulching is that it prevents the soil from being compacted by drip from overhead trees.

In general, woodlanders prefer organic fertilizers to those of purely chemical origin. Use, therefore, bone meal and dried blood, tankage, cotton-seed meal and the like rather than commercial fertilizers made for vegetable and flower gardens.

Among woodland plants are a number that are exceedingly finicky about the exact degree of the acidity of the soil—the mayflower and many wild orchids, for example. If you want to grow these you must study their particular needs.

The Plants. In addition to shade loving plants—those kinds that really need shade—there are many plants that are shade tolerant. These grow well in sun but will stand more or less shade if the soil and situation are otherwise favorable. Such plants are excellent for places that get full sun for part of the day and shade for the remainder and spots that get filtered sun.

Allow more distance between plants set out in the shade than you do when planting sunny gardens. That is how nature does it. If you follow her lead your planting in the shade will look more convincing and be more satisfying. Well spaced plants benefit from more side light and more reflected light than do crowded specimens. They can spread their foliage wider to collect the fullest amount of light from above.

Hotbeds and Cold-Frames

✣✣

Install a cold-frame and, if possible, some form of heated glass structure in your garden. You can then raise many of the plants you need both economically and easily. The heated structure may be a greenhouse, a frame warmed by hot water, steam, electricity, or a vent from the cellar, or it may be a frame containing a bed of soil, called a hotbed, warmed by electricity or fermenting manure.

In a greenhouse you can grow a great variety of plants throughout the entire year. A heated frame is grand for preserving such plants as geraniums, lantanas, and heliotropes through the winter and for raising young vegetables and flower-garden plants in the spring. Hotbeds and cold-frames are most useful for the spring protection of vegetables and flowers that need an early start—tomatoes, snapdragons, and petunias for example, and for preserving through the winter many other plants.

Biennials such as canterbury bells and English wallflowers are wintered in cold-frames in the North as well as newly propagated shrubs, evergreens, and rock garden plants. Any of these glass structures gives you an opportunity to propagate a great many plants by means of cuttings.

Under special circumstances, for instance, when cool summer conditions are sought for violets or primroses,

A modern way to glaze cold-frames is to tack or staple sheet butyrate plastic to each sash, trim with razor.

A cold-frame glazed with plastic is light, easy to move, and shatterproof. And the glazing job is simple.

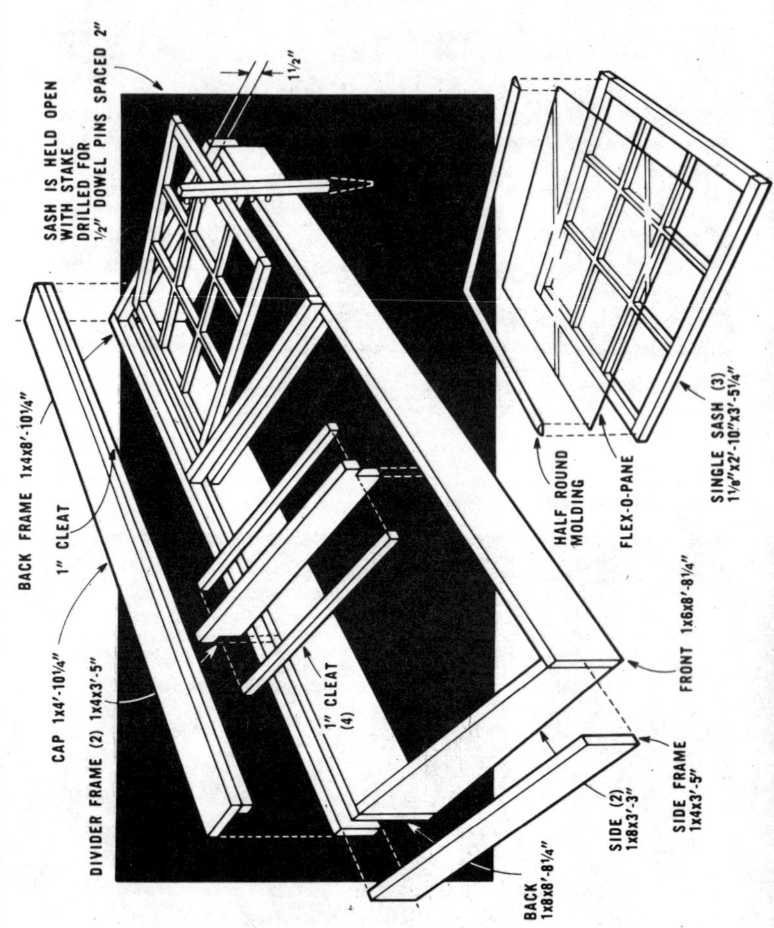

Plan for an easy-to-build cold-frame.

cold-frames are faced to the north but nearly always they, like the hotbeds, are faced as nearly due south as possible. Choose a sheltered place for both frames and hotbeds. Cold, sweeping winds are harmful.

Correct ventilating is most important with all glass structures. Take care that the temperatures inside do not build up rapidly so that the plants are harmed. On the other hand, the sudden admission of any considerable volume of cold air to a frame containing tender plants is highly dangerous. In cold weather ventilate gradually. Open the sash just a tiny crack to begin with, more as the day warms up. Close down gradually in the afternoon or evening. In mild weather ventilation may be left on all night.

Do not keep frames that contain hardy plants too warm during the day, even in winter. Plenty of ventilation whenever the temperature is above freezing should be the rule. On very cold nights cover the sash with wooden shutters, blanket-like covers, or mats made of straw or reeds. These are important over hotbeds.

How to Sow Seeds

To grow, seeds must have moisture, warmth, and air. In addition, they must be alive. Some lose their vitality within a few weeks of ripening, others are good for many years. Most are reliable for twelve months from the time they are gathered, then gradually deteriorate.

Seeds of bog plants and water plants usually die if they become really dry. Store them in moist moss or in water. These are capable of obtaining the oxygen they need from water. Other seeds are not. Therefore, it is fatal to sow those of ordinary land plants in waterlogged soil. Good drainage is essential. Each soil particle should be surrounded by a film of moisture. The spaces between should contain air. This necessitates good subsurface drainage and watering as often as is necessary to replenish moisture lost by evaporation. It is fatal to let the soil dry just at the time the seeds are sprouting. Desiccation is rapidly followed by death.

Timeliness. Choose the times of sowing your seeds carefully. Consider especially temperatures and the number of growing days available. It is useless to sow certain crops (lima beans and cucumbers for example) while the soil is yet cold; it is difficult or impossible to persuade seeds of many perennials to germinate during extreme summer heat. Those annuals that die in hot, humid

For sowing in drills, rake soil fine, measure off drill intervals, and stretch guide cord. Draw hoe along cord to make drill: hoe handle makes a shallow one. Soak drill with water, then scatter seed thinly. After covering seed press earth down and roughen it slightly.

weather must be sown early so that they will bloom before this comes along. Biennials sown too late will not produce plants large enough to be satisfactory. Adjust the sowing dates of plants raised early indoors so that they are the right size for planting outdoors when planting time comes along. Timeliness is of the first importance to successful seed sowing.

Soils. In order that seeds may be assured sufficient air, prepare the soil so that it is crumbly and porous. Clayey soils cake at the surface and seal off the air.

For indoor sowing use soil consisting of about equal parts of medium-heavy top soil, coarse sand and peat moss or leaf mold. If the topsoil is heavy, increase the proportions of sand and humus, if distinctly sandy reduce the amount of sand added.

Let the soil be reasonably fine but not excessively so. Its fineness should be in relation to the size of the seeds. Large seeds such as sweet peas and beans may be sown in coarser soil than radishes and stocks, and for these latter the earth may be less fine than for extremely small seeds such as lobelias and begonias.

When sowing indoors, sift the soil through a three quarter inch mesh. Use this for filling the body of the pots or flats. For small seeds, top off the flats or pots with a half inch layer passed through a half inch mesh. For very fine seeds pass the surface soil through a quarter inch mesh, or even through mosquito screening.

Prepare outdoor seed beds by forking them and making the surface reasonably fine and quite level. Then, when the soil is moderately moist (never when it is wet and sticky) compact it moderately by treading it. With a rake work the upper two or three inches of soil back and forth until it is really fine.

It is very important to catch the soil in just the right condition for early sowings. Often, following a sunny or breezy period it will be in just the right condition and then rain will change matters entirely and seed sowing may not be possible for another week or two. Take advantage of every opportunity the weather affords.

Seed Sowing Indoors. Seeds sown indoors are accommodated in flats (shallow boxes), pots, or pans (shallow flower pots). These should be clean. They must be provided with drainage holes. Place an inch or so of coarse cinders or broken pieces of flower pots over the drainage holes. On top of this spread a thin layer of coarse leaves or moss. Then fill nearly to the top with the prepared soil, pressed moderately firmly with the finger tips. Let the finished surface be slightly lower than the rim of the container and perfectly level. Before scattering the seed, water the soil thoroughly. Use boiling water if possible. Apply it in the form of a fine spray. Let it drain for ten or fifteen minutes before sowing.

Scatter the seeds evenly (the distance between seeds should be about four times their average diameter). Press them lightly into the surface. Sift fine soil over them to a depth of once or twice their diameters. Extremely fine seeds such as lobelias and begonias need no soil covering. Label the receptacles. Cover them with sheets of glass over which paper is laid, and place where they are to germinate. The temperature needed varies somewhat according to kind, but the majority of commonly grown plants succeed between fifty-five and sixty-five degrees.

Examine daily until the plants appear. Quick germinating seeds will need no watering during this period. Those that come up slower will probably require attention. Never permit the soil to dry. As soon as you can see the young plants, remove the glass and paper. Protect from bright sunlight with paper or cheesecloth. Use a fine syringe to keep the surface soil moist. Water thoroughly whenever necessary by immersion or by spray.

As the plants develop they push their roots deeper into the soil. Maintaining the surface in a constantly moist condition is then of less importance—in fact it is rather advantageous to have it somewhat on the dry side during spells of dull weather. Do not, however, let the entire body of soil dry out.

Seed Sowing Outdoors and In Frames. Outdoors, seeds are sown either where the plants are to mature or in beds or frames from which the young plants are later transplanted. When sowing where the plants are to remain, incorporate manure and fertilizer. Do not do this when making a nursery-bed.

Seeds are broadcast by scattering them evenly over the entire area, or are planted in drills (rows) or in hills (groups). The broadcast method is used for lawns and for some annuals. It is more wasteful of seed than the other methods and it adds to the difficulty of weeding and cultivating. Seeds which are broadcast are worked into the soil by lightly raking the surface back and forth. Following this, the surface is firmed either by pressing it with a board, tamping it lightly with flat side of the head of a hoe, or by using the garden roller.

The drill method involves making shallow furrows. Let their depth vary according to the soil (on light soils sow more deeply than on heavy soils) and according to the type of seed being sown. It is usual to sow seeds at from two to four times their own diameter. When sowings are made early in the year while the soil is cold, sow somewhat more shallowly than for later sowings. Soak the drills before sowing with a slowly flowing stream from a hose or watering can. This pre-watering is a much better method than the more common practice of sowing first and watering afterwards, which may cake the surface. Scatter the seeds thinly and evenly along the bottoms of the drills. Cover by pulling over them with the rake some of the soil from along the sides of the drill. Then firm lightly with the back of the rake or hoe and rake the whole surface very lightly and in the same direction as the drills. Do not disturb the seeds.

When sowing in hills, it is usual to make a low mound at each station by pulling together the surface soil with a hoe. Into the top of each of these "hills" a shallow depression is made and several seeds are sown in this and are then covered with soil. Sometimes mounds are dispensed with and a shallow depression is drawn with a hoe at each plant station. Several seeds are scattered in each depression and are covered with soil. Seeds sown out-of-doors or in frames should be labeled in the same manner as those sown indoors.

Raising Plants from Cuttings

It is a simple matter to propagate many kinds of plants from cuttings or slips. Some, such as sedums, are so easy that scraps which lie on the ground root spontaneously. A few, such as lilacs, are difficult even for professional propagators. Between are the geraniums, begonias, red currants, privets and hundreds of others that are easy to root if given just a little care.

The kinds of cuttings most commonly used are leafy stem-cuttings, hardwood-cuttings, and root-cuttings.

Leafy Stem Cuttings. The housewife who keeps a shoot of English ivy in a glass of water or who plants a rose "slip" in summer under a Mason jar and in this way raises new plants is propagating by means of leafy stem cuttings.

The techniques she employs or modifications of them are used to secure increase of thousands of kinds of popular plants—geraniums, begonias, lantanas, heliotropes, fuchsias, carnations and chrysanthemums among flower garden favorites, numerous kinds of shrubs, evergreens and vines, and such groundcovers as vinca, pachysandra, and trailing roses.

Leafy stems of most (but not all) garden plants can be induced to root if they are taken at the right season and are kept under suitable conditions. Some, such as begonias, root readily anytime. Others, including most

When sand is used as the rooting medium, pack it down before inserting leafy cuttings. Use a blunt dibble to make planting holes, then firm sand around roots with the end of the dibble. Water plants with a fine spray.

shrubs and evergreens, only when the wood is just right.

When you remove a leafy shoot from its parent you immediately cut it off from its supply of water (its roots). Yet its leaves continue to give out moisture. If this loss is not replaced the shoot dies. Your first concern then must be to check excessive water loss from your cuttings; your second to make it possible for the cuttings to obtain moisture.

To avoid excessive loss, keep cuttings which cannot be planted immediately wrapped in polyethylene plastic film or moist newspaper. Also, remove the leaves from the part of the cutting that will be buried when it is planted. If the cuttings are decidedly leafy, cut off some of their upper foliage, remove some entire leaves and, if they are big like hydrangeas, cut off part of each large leaf that is left. Maintain a moist atmosphere. To do this, set the cuttings in a greenhouse, cold-frame, terrarium, or under a belljar, Mason jar or cover them with a polyethylene bag. Avoid drafts. Give a little ventilation—at first only just enough to keep the air from being dripping wet—somewhat more as the cuttings establish themselves, but never enough to cause the foliage to wilt. After roots have formed, gradually accustom the young plants to normal air conditions. Sprinkle the cuttings lightly with a very fine spray of water once, twice or more times a day, but never so late that they are wet when night falls. Shade lightly from direct sunshine.

To encourage and make it possible for the cuttings to absorb moisture, plant them in a medium such as coarse sand, sand and peat moss, perlite or vermiculite that insures a supply of air to the roots as well as moisture. Many cuttings will root in water but in almost all cases water is not to be preferred. Keep the medium always evenly moist, not constantly saturated. This necessitates good drainage underneath. Except in the case of vermiculite and perlite, make the medium firm before planting, and firm it well about the newly set cuttings, particularly about their bases. Leave vermiculite and perlite loose.

Make sure that the base of each cutting rests on the bottom of the hole in which it is placed for rooting.

Your cuttings will root better if you cut their bases just beneath a node (joint). Slice across the stem horizontally with a keen knife.

Most cuttings root quicker if the rooting medium is kept five or ten degrees warmer than the average air temperature. This is not necessary, however, except with a few distinctly finicky kinds.

When inserting cuttings space them so that they scarcely touch each other. After planting, remove promptly any decayed leaves or parts of leaves that develop.

Polyethylene plastic film (the kind freezer bags are made of) can be used to root cuttings. A propagator can be made by taking a wooden box, 4 in. deep and as long and broad as convenient, and boring holes in its bottom for drainage. An inch of cinders or gravel is placed over the bottom and then the box is filled nearly to its top with firmly packed moist sand or vermiculite (not packed).

A framework is then erected that will support a plastic covering so that it covers top, sides, and ends of the box and is at such a height above the box that it does not touch the cuttings. The framework can be of wire (old coat hangers may be adapted for the purpose) or of canes or wood.

After the cuttings are inserted, place a layer of damp cheesecloth over the framework, and cover with a sheet of polyethelene plastic. These coverings should fit snugly so that drying drafts can not enter.

The other way of using polyethylene film to root cuttings is simply to take several cuttings after they are made, wrap sphagnum moss around their bases, and enclose them in a bag of polyethylene. Keep them where temperature and other conditions are favorable and leave them until roots are produced, when they may be potted or planted individually in sandy soil.

Hardwood Cuttings. If you cut a twig from a privet in the fall and leave it on the ground it will dry and die. If you prevent it from drying it will live and, under suitable conditions, will develop roots, shoots, and form a new plant in spring. So will many other deciduous shrubs. That is the basis of propagation by hardwood cuttings.

Make hardwood cuttings in fall after the leaves have dropped. Select firm, strong shoots that developed during the current year—that is, that grew during the summer just closed. Cut these into pieces each six to ten inches long. Slice the base of each across horizontally just beneath a node and cut its top slantwise just above a node.

Tie the prepared cuttings in bundles with soft string, with their bases all at one end. Let each bundle contain up to fifty cuttings. Label them.

Bury the bundles in sand in a cold-frame or out-of-doors, letting them rest either horizontally or with their bases upwards. Cover with sand to a depth of six or eight inches and later, after the surface has frozen, throw a layer of hay or leaves over it. The idea is to prevent the cuttings from actually freezing. In spring, well before the trees open their buds, dig the cuttings up and plant them individually in rows in a nicely prepared nursery bed.

At the time you lift the cuttings their bases will be well calloused and in many cases they will have developed promising young roots. Don't let them dry.

With a spade, open a narrow trench that has one side nearly vertical and is of such a depth that when the base of a cutting rests on its bottom its upper-end protrudes not more than an inch above the surface.

Set the cuttings in the trench, leaning them against the nearly vertical side and space them three to four inches apart. Fill the trench with sandy soil and tread it firmly. In heavy soils an inch of coarse sand on the bottom of the trench is helpful.

If you are setting more than one row of cuttings, allow sufficient space between to permit you to cultivate. Don't allow the soil to become really dry at any time. Water thoroughly when necessary.

During the summer, hardwood cuttings make substantial growth. The following spring dig the young plants up, prune them back fairly severely, and transplant them to a nursery bed where they can develop further. In the nursery allow them more room than they had in the cutting bed.

Among popular plants that are easily propagated by hardwood cuttings are: deutzia, weigelia, mock orange, snowberry, coralberry, forsythia, euonymus, viburnum, spirea, shrubby dogwoods, firethorn, franklinia, bladdernut, willows, poplars, honeysuckles, climbing roses, beautyberry, vitex, rose of Sharon, grapes, gooseberry, currants, and mulberry.

Root Cuttings. Some plants can be easily increased by using pieces of root as cuttings. Horseradish, for example, and pachysandra, trumpet creeper, Japanese anemones, and blackberries.

Select fat roots, cut them into pieces each two to four inches long, and plant them in sandy soil or cold-frames outdoors, or in beds of peat moss and sand indoors.

Make root cuttings fairly late in the fall. If they are to be raised indoors, plant them immediately in the propagating bed. Keep them cool at first, somewhat warmer after a month or six weeks. If they are to be planted outside, store them until spring in peat moss and sand in a temperature of about 40 degrees, and then plant them in frames or in the garden. You may winter root cuttings by burying them in sand outdoors provided they are protected from hard freezing. If planted indoors, pot the young plants when they have developed sufficiently, if outdoors, transplant the following spring.

Cuttings of many plants root more quickly and certainly if you treat them with a root-inducing hormone before planting. Follow the manufacturers' directions when using these preparations.

How to Divide Plants

⚘⚘

Dividing or separating is the simplest of all vegetative propagation. It's just a matter of splitting one large plant into two or more smaller ones. Each division or separation, if planted under conditions suitable to its kind, grows.

Divide plants not only to obtain increase but also to reduce the size of those that have become too large; also to prevent crowding and consequent weakening of the stems within the clumps themselves.

Some fast-growing perennials need dividing every year or two. Others thrive for many years undisturbed. So with bulbs. The best rule to follow is to dig them up, separate them, and grade and replant them when they begin to show signs of deteriorating.

Basic points about dividing plants are (1) Discard those affected with viruses or other incurable or difficult-to-cure conditions. (2) Separate bulbs that are to be stored for the summer, such as tulips, at lifting time; all other plants at the beginning of a period of active root growth. Thus you will divide most hardy perennials and certain shrubs in early fall or in spring. Irises, oriental poppies, and some others that begin a new cycle of root growth in summer at that time. Primroses and a good many other spring-blooming perennials may be successfully divided immediately after they have bloomed. Divide dahlias, cannas, and plants that are wintered in storage just before they are started into new growth in spring.

When dividing perennials or shrubs, see that each division has a generous amount of roots as well as some plump buds or top growth. Usually the most vigorous parts of shrubs and perennials are the younger portions that form the outsides of the old clumps. Save these parts and discard the centers unless you want rapid increase.

A good, sharp spade or a hatchet are satisfactory tools with which to split shrubs. Some of the more vigorous perennials can be divided in like manner but I prefer to cut most into pieces with a heavy, sharp knife or to pull them apart either with the hands or by thrusting a pair of forks back to back closely together well down into their roots and then prying apart.

With a little practice you will be able to separate even the more difficult kinds such as peonies, Christmas roses, and coralbells without much trouble. Do not let the divisions dry out. Plant them promptly.

There is little danger that herbaceous plants divided when they are without leaves or when their new growth is only just beginning will, after planting, lose moisture faster than their roots can replace it. But this is not true of plants divided when in leaf, as evergreens must be, and some other plants are. These face a real danger of death by desiccation.

To prevent this employ the following practices. (1) When you prepare the divisions for planting, cut back the foliage, thus reducing the leaf area from which moisture is lost. Leafage may be reduced from one third to two thirds in most cases. (2) Retain the maximum amount of roots possible with each division. (3) If possible select moist, dull weather for planting. (4) Shade from bright sunshine and protect from drying winds for a few days or a week or two after planting. (5) Water the foliage lightly several times daily.

In special cases it is greatly advantageous to plant leafy divisions in a shaded cold-frame and to keep this closed or sparsely ventilated until the young plants have recovered from the shock of dividing. This prevents excessive loss of moisture from the leaves.

Deciduous shrubs, even if divided when dormant, may soon produce more leafage than their roots can support. It is a good plan to cut the stems of such divisions severely back before they are planted, or to thin the stems out thoroughly.

Keep the soil in which newly planted divisions are planted moist but not constantly saturated. Remember, roots need air as well as moisture.

Some plants, such as red raspberries, send up sucker growths some little distance away from the main clump. The digging up and transplanting of these is a form of division.

Increase Plants by Layering

✣✣✣

If you snip a piece off a plant and induce it to form roots you are propagating by cuttings. If you cause roots to form on the piece first and then snip it off you are propagating by layering. Some plants layer themselves. Branches of forsythias and blackberries, for example, take root and give rise to new plants. Strawberries send out runners which bear plantlets that root into the ground.

You can increase many kinds of plants by layering—lilacs, rhododendrons, wisterias, magnolias, hollies, junipers, yews, quinces, hydrangeas and many roses, for instance.

To layer strawberries and other plants that produce runners, fill three-inch pots with good, sandy soil. Remove all but four or five strong runners from each vigorous plant. Cut the ends off these just beyond the first young plantlet. Sink the pots to their rims in the soil. Place a plantlet on top of each pot and peg it down with a wire peg or staple. Keep the soil moist. When the plantlets have rooted freely into their pots cut the runners between them and their parents. About a week later transplant them from their pots to permanent beds. That is the simplest type of layering.

The next easiest is tip-layering. This is used for blackberries, black raspberries, loganberries, and similar plants. Bend a cane over in summer and bury its tip to a depth of

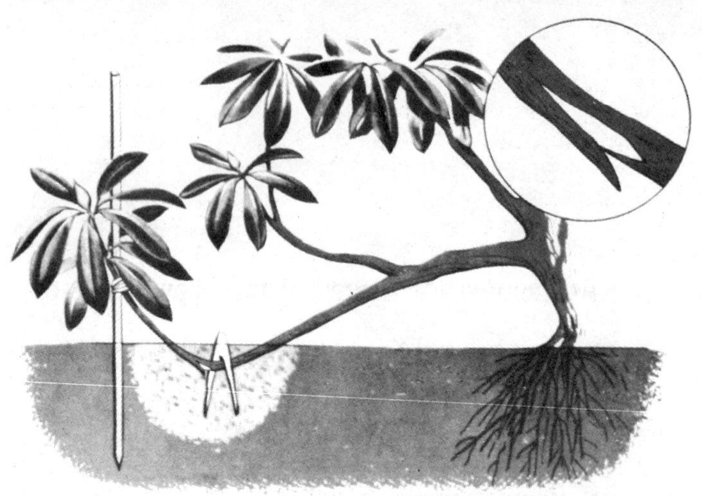

Rhododendron plant with branch held under the soil with a forked stick to induce rooting at the injured point (*see circle*). Injured part is in sandy, peaty soil. At the end of two years snip layered branch off parent. Transplant.

about three inches in the soil, pegging or weighting it so that it cannot spring out. Keep the soil moist. A new plant soon forms. In late fall or in spring cut the young plant free from its parent. Transplant it in spring.

Ordinary layering consists of burying a portion of a stem some little way behind its tip in soil. The end of the shoot itself sticks out and develops into a new plant when the buried portion forms roots. This is how to do it:

In spring or early summer select one-year-old branches of healthy rhododendrons, magnolias, hollies or almost any kind of tree or shrub having branches which will bend to the ground. Loosen the soil and mix with peat moss. If it is heavy, mix in some coarse sand. If very poor, dig out two or three shovelsful and replace it with a mixture of good topsoil, peat moss, and sand.

Before you put the branch out into the soil, injure it in some way at the point that will be underground. This partly checks the sap flow and aids root development.

The needed injury can be done in one of various ways. You may grasp the stem in both hands and give it a sturdy half twist so that the bark loosens or breaks from the underlying wood. Or take a sharp knife and cut the stem a little below a node. Cut upwards toward the tip. Make the cut an inch or so long, and let it extend to a depth of one third the thickness of the branch. Yet another method is to split the branch with a chisel and then peg the slit open with a small wooden wedge.

Bury the injured part of the stem in sandy, peaty soil—to a depth of four or six inches if it is a branch of a sturdy shrub, not more than an inch or two if it is a smaller plant such as an evergreen candytuft. Peg it in place with forked twigs or long wire staples and, if needed, drive a stake into the ground and tie the end of the branch that sticks out of the soil to it. Make sure that the layer is firmly anchored. It must not be loose. Keep soil moist.

Polyethylene Plastic Film. Polyethylene plastic film is the kind used for making bags in which food in deep freezers

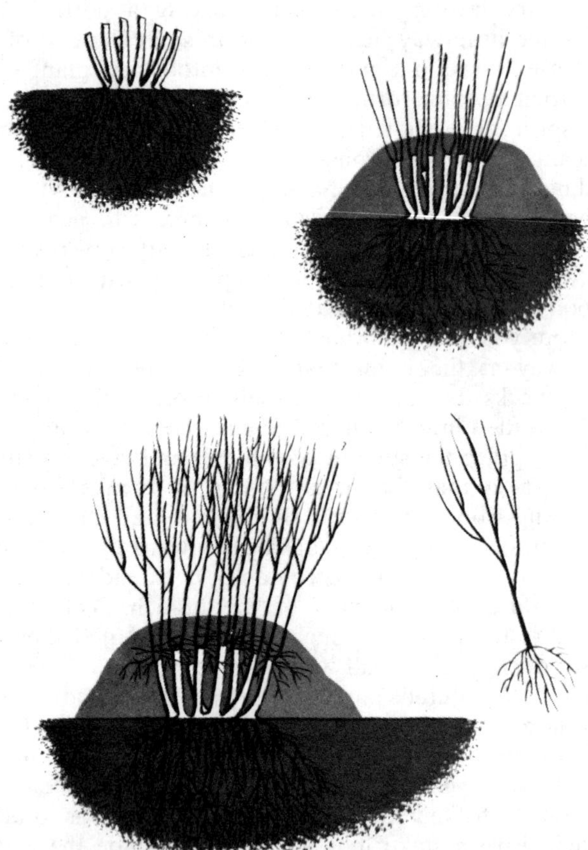

In mound layering, cut back shrubs in the spring and mound sandy soil over old stubs as shown. New shoots will root into the mound, can be cut off as individual shrubs.

is kept. It possesses the remarkable property of permitting gases, such as air, to pass through it freely but of stopping the passage of moisture. This makes it valuable for use in certain plant propagation techniques. It is possible to secure increase of many kinds of plants that heretofore presented special difficulties without the use of a greenhouse and to increase plants outdoors in ways not hitherto practicable.

For the production of roots on layered branches, the maintenance of humid conditions about the parts from which the roots are to develop, together with free access of air, is absolutely necessary. By wrapping the critical parts in polyethylene film these conditions are assured. Here's how.

Wound the branch to be rooted where the wood is firm, but not too far from the tip of the branch; about a foot away is usually a suitable distance. The wound may be made by removing a half-inch-wide ring of bark completely around the stem or by making a cut into the stem in an upward direction for an inch or two and extending nearly to its center. Peg the cut open with a thin sliver of wood. Wrap around the wounded part a good handful or two of sphagnum moss that has been soaked in water and squeezed as dry as possible. Press the moss firmly about the stem and wrap it securely in polyethylene film. Secure it at the top and bottom with ties wrapped over with electrician's tape to keep rain out.

Within a month or two roots from the wounded stem will show on the outside of the moss ball and can be seen through the plastic. When these appear the rooted branch is cut from the parent, the plastic is removed, and the branch is planted in a pot of sandy soil. Until the roots permeate the soil, the young plant should be kept out of winds and sun, preferably in a close cold-frame or covered by an inverted bottomless box with a sheet of glass or of polyethylene plastic covering the top. When new roots have filled the pot the plant may be planted outdoors.

How to Graft and Bud

Grafting is the joining together of two living plant parts to form a permanent union. The part that includes the roots is called the stock. The part grafted on to the stock is the scion. Budding is a form of grafting in which the scion consists of a single bud.

There is nothing mysterious about grafting. You may do it yourself in your own garden once you master the simple principles. These are (1) Stock and scion must be closely related botanically. You can graft a garden rose on to a wild rose, or a Delicious apple on to a seedling apple. Stock and scion in each case belong to the same genus. You can even graft a pear tree on to a quince or a lilac on to a privet. Here stocks and scions belong to the same botanical families. But you cannot graft a lilac onto a quince, an apple onto a privet, or a cherry onto an oak because in these cases stocks and scions are not related closely enough.

(2) The cambium layers of stock and scion must be brought into close contact. The cambium is a thin layer of actively growing tissue between wood and bark.

(3) Stock and scion must be bound together to prevent movement and be prevented from drying at point of graft.

(4) Grafting is done in spring just before active growth begins. Budding is done in summer.

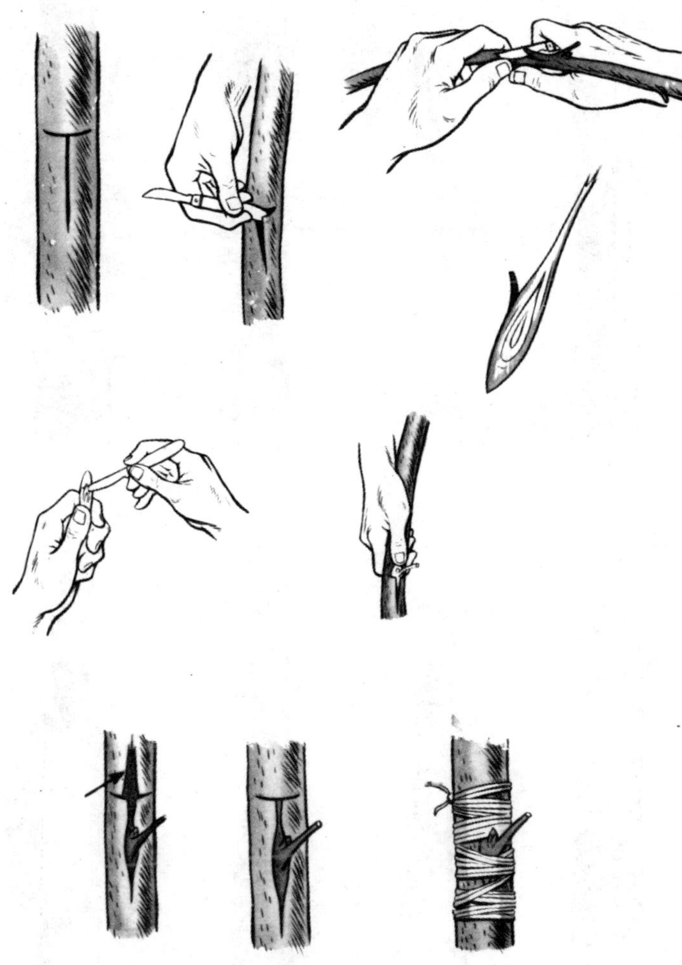

First step in budding is to make a T-shaped cut one inch long in the bark of the stock. Lift bark away from wood. Then cut a bud from a budstick leaving a tail of bark. Pick out wood adhering to bud. Slide bud into incision. The tail of bark should protrude as shown; trim it flush and tie bud to stock with cotton tape or raffia.

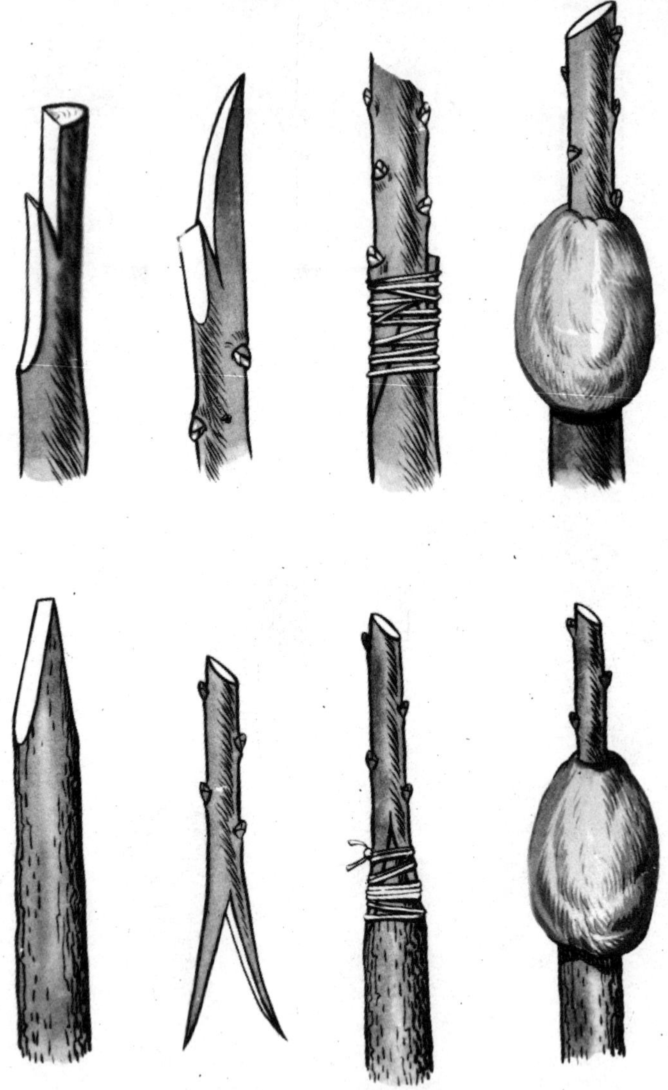

Whip grafting *(top)* and saddle grafting — two ways of joining scion to stock. Grafting wax seals grafts.

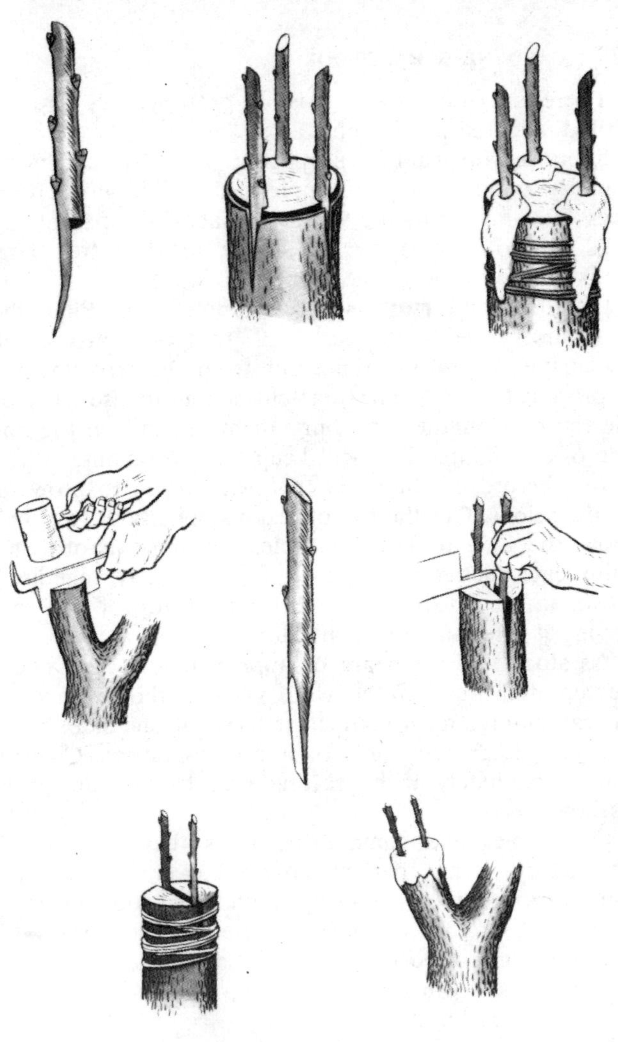

Rind grafting *(top)* and cleft grafting *(bottom)* are used when the stock is much larger than the scion.

There are numerous kinds of grafting. We are concerned with the most useful.

Suppose you want to propagate young trees of a particularly good variety of apple. Seeds will not produce trees that have fruit the same as that of the parent. Cuttings will not root. You can't divide an apple tree. Grafting is the way to raise the plants you want.

Obtain one-year-old, seedling, apple trees. Plant them in a nursery bed in the early fall. In spring, two or three weeks before grafting time, cut from the tree you want to propagate strong one-year-old shoots to use as scions. Tie these in bundles and bury them in sand on the north side of a building. This will keep them dormant.

Just before the buds on the stock begin to grow take up the scions. Cut the top off each stock about two inches above the ground. Then with clean slicing cuts of a sharp knife cut stock and scion to fit accurately together as shown in the illustrations. Also cut the top off the scion, leaving it three or four inches long.

As stock and scion are of approximately the same diameter, make use of the whip graft method. Make sure the cambiums are in contact at least on one side. Tie securely together with raffia or thin cotton strips. Cover the graft immediately with grafting wax to exclude air and insects.

Old apples and some other trees that are not of a satisfactory variety can be changed over to another by "top working" them—cutting them back and grafting on to the stubs scions of desired varieties. Cleft grafting or rind grafting is used here.

Peaches and other "stone" fruits and roses are usually propagated by budding.

For scions or budwood use strong shoots of the current season's growth that have well-developed buds. Cut off the leaves. To insert a bud, follow the steps shown in the drawings.

Give Your Plants Winter Protection

⚘⚘

Don't think of winter protection merely as a matter of keeping plants warm. It's not that simple. Temperatures are important but other factors are, too.

Alternating thawing and freezing may do far more harm than steady cold. Winds and strong sun late in winter may be more disastrous than winter cold. Snow lying for long periods often counterbalances low temperatures. Plants on poorly drained or heavy soils are more likely to suffer than are those on lighter or porous soils. Very rich soil may bring lush, poorly ripened growth more likely to winter-kill than the firmer growth made on rather leaner soils. Attacks by insects or diseases, improper pruning, and other cultural faults can all increase susceptibility to winter-injury.

Well, what to do about it? Take really tender plants such as geraniums and begonias indoors, also such summer bulbs as cannas and gladioli.

Slightly tender plants that are small may be wintered in cold-frames. In cold-frames, too, you may carry over young potted trees and shrubs, perennials, and rock garden plants. "Slightly tender" covers different plants in different localities. Local experience is your best guide. In New York, pansies and Canterbury bells are in this category. But what about plants that must be left outdoors?

Hybrid tea roses with tops cut back and soil heaped to a height of eight inches (minimum) around bases.

Fig trees and other tender, deciduous plants can be wrapped in straw, burlap, or waterproof paper.

We can protect their roots and tops with mulches.

Mulching the soil surface reduces the depth to which frost penetrates and minimizes the bad effects of alternate freezing and thawing. In a way it is a substitute for a winter-long snow covering.

Use almost any loose organic material, littery manure, leaves, salt hay, peat moss, corn stalks, straw, pine needles, or the like. Let the mulch be two to six inches deep. Do not apply it until the upper inch or two of the soil has frozen and winter has definitely arrived.

Be particularly careful not to cover the tops of plants that stay green all winter, such an foxgloves, evergreen candytuft, and pinks, with a heavy layer. Mulch the soil about them and cover their tops very lightly with something that admits air but does not mat down. Branches of evergreens such as pine and fir are suitable. So are salt hay, straw, and corn stalks. Place a few pieces of brushwood over the plants before you spread these last mentioned coverings.

Protect evergreens likely to suffer from "winter-burn" by mulching heavily, by erecting windbreaks on the north, northeast and northwest, and by shading from strong sun. Windbreaks and shading may be made of laths nailed closely together on a framework or by burlap screens. Invert bushel baskets over small specimens. Another good way with evergreens is to stick branches of evergreens that retain their needles when cut (pine and fir) into the ground around them, or to stand evergreen branches against the plant to be protected and tie them into place.

Do something about deciduous, woody plants tender enough to be harmed by severe cold. Roses and French hydrangeas are in this category in many sections. So are figs in climates like New York City. The problem is to keep the branches from exposure to excessively low temperatures.

You can do this by burying them in the soil. Climbing roses, tree roses, and figs that have their branches trained close to the ground may be laid down and covered. After the soil has frozen, mulch with straw or leaves. Draw mounds of soil to a height of eight inches around hybrid tea roses. Mulch after it has frozen. It does not matter if the upper parts of the canes are killed because they are pruned away in spring.

Another way of protecting stems susceptible to cold is to wrap them in layers of straw, corn stalks, or burlap, and enclose this in a wrapping of polyethylene plastic film or heavy, waterproof paper.

If you drain your water-lily pool, move the tubs together and cover with straw or leaves to prevent freezing. Small pools may be left undrained if bridged across with boards and well covered with mulch. Hardy aquatics may then be left in place. Hardy water lilies may be left in pools if they are deep enough so that their roots will not freeze. Float a few logs or empty barrels on the water to take up the expansion as it freezes.

Save evergreens and any deciduous trees and shrubs that are in danger of breakage from accumulations of snow, particularly of snow that is wet, heavy, and likely to freeze. With a wooden rake shake the branches gently. Watch out for snow slides from roots on to foundation planting.

Don't remove winter protection too early in spring. Wait until the buds are ready to grow. Uncover gradually and during dull, moist weather if possible.

How to Prune

✣✣

Pruning is an acquired art. Without adequate understanding, men are apt to commit a kind of tree and shrub butchery in its name while ladies are likely to approach their victims with such tender hearts that the few pathetic snips they make are ineffective.

Pruning needs intelligent understanding. Never cut off a limb or branch without having an entirely good reason for doing so.

Prune out dead branches without hesitation. Remove also those infected with diseases that call for this treatment as well as branches severely infested with scale insects. But beyond that consider carefully before you cut. Always use sharp tools.

The kind of pruning needed may vary at different periods in the life of a plant. Many shrubs and trees benefit from being cut back rather severely at planting time. During their early years trees, vines, and shrubs trained to particular habits require formative pruning. Most fruits and some ornamental trees and shrubs need pruning as part of the annual routine.

Rejuvenation Pruning. This is a drastic, but effective, way of restoring neglected shrubs of many kinds which are tall, straggly, and bare-bottomed. Simply cut the specimen

Crossing shoots growing from branches of fruit trees should not be permitted to crowd the center part.

down to within a few inches of the ground in early spring. Then feed it liberally with manure and bone meal or with a balanced commercial fertilizer. Water thoroughly and repeatedly if the weather is dry. At the end of the first season you will have a very respectable and shapely young shrub.

Not all kinds respond to this treatment. Among those that do are spireas, mock oranges, deutzias, weigelias, viburnums, snowberry, Indian currant, lilacs, privets, honeysuckles, shrubby dogwoods, tamarix, and barberries. If you cut down grafted lilacs or other shrubs propagated in this way be careful that the shoots that grow and are allowed to remain do not arise from the worthless understock.

Most broad leaved evergreens respond to rejuvenation pruning. Rhododendrons, mountain laurel, true laurel, hollies, and aucuba are examples. Yews may be cut back severely too.

Shade Trees. Prune young shade trees to encourage them to develop strong adequate frameworks not subject to storm damage and branched rather high up. Remove unwanted branches before they thicken.

Eliminate weak crotches. These occur when the central shoot of a young tree divides into two shoots of about equal thickness or when a strong side shoot develops and grows upwards almost parallel with the central shoot. If these equal leaders are allowed to develop the tree is very likely to eventually tear apart at the point where the two branches meet. In old trees this danger can be greatly lessened by bolting or cabling the limbs together. It is better to avoid this necessity by preventing the development of such danger points. Do this by cutting out one branch of the crotch before it exceeds pencil thickness.

Cut out the least important of each pair of crossing branches. If one branch grows much faster than the others, shorten it while yet young to preserve the general shapeliness of the tree.

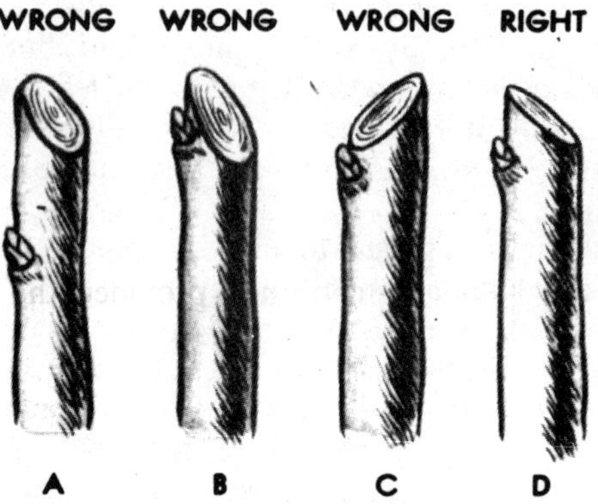

Three wrong ways to prune and one right way. *A* is too far above bud. *B* is started too low and *C* has low side of cut on the side bearing the bud. *D* is the right way.

When pruning rose bushes make clean, sloping cuts just above buds with slope pointing the way the new shoots will grow. Wear gloves and use sharp tools.

When it comes to pruning large trees—work that involves climbing and perhaps the removal of heavy branches—hire a qualified expert on a contract basis. Don't do it yourself and don't let anyone unskilled in tree surgery do it. Slips and mistakes may result in serious injury or be fatal.

Contrary to common belief, it doesn't matter what time of year shade trees are pruned provided the temperature is not so low that the wood is frozen and brittle. Maples, birches, mulberries, and some others "bleed" profusely if pruned in spring. This looks alarming. It does no appreciable harm. To avoid bleeding prune in summer.

Stubs should never be left when pruning. Cut branches flush with the trunk or branch from which they originate. Take off heavy limbs by first making an undercut a few inches away from the main trunk or branch. Then overcut a couple of inches outward from the undercut until the branch is off. Then saw off flush the short stump that remains. Cover all wounds with tree-wound paint.

Deciduous Flowering Shrubs and Trees. These fall into two classes. (1) Those that bloom on branches a year or more old. (2) Those that bloom on current season's wood. Forsythia is a good example of (1), rose of Sharon of (2).

Cut back severely in winter or spring, rose of Sharon flowers the same year, forsythia does not. Learn precisely which shrubs belong to which class before you prune.

You can not generalize. French hydrangeas belong to (1), peegee hydrangea to (2); bridal wreath spirea to (1), Anthony Waterer spirea to (2); alternate-leaved butterfly bush to (1), common butterfly bush to (2); rambler roses to (1), hybrid tea roses to (2) and so on.

Most shrubs that flower on previous year's wood do so in spring or early summer. You may prune them immediately after they have bloomed by cutting out all thin, weak shoots, ill-placed branches, and as many old flowering stems as necessary to assure the new growths

PRUNING SHOULD BEGIN ON YOUNG TREES ~

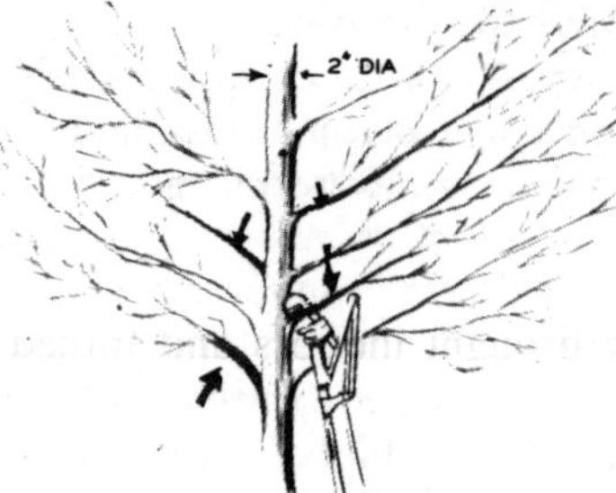

MANY SMALL BRANCHES TRY TO SPROUT CROWDING OUT EACH OTHER - THIN OUT BY CUTTING

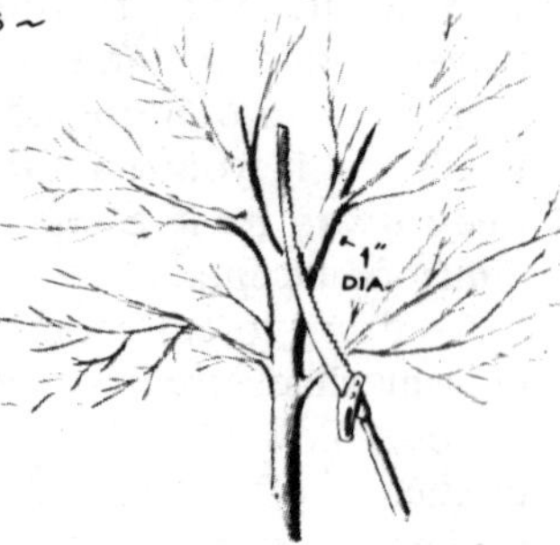

DO NOT LET MAIN TRUNK DIVIDE INTO FORK, WEAKENS TREE. REMOVE ONE BRANCH

REMOVE DEAD LIMBS QUICKLY ~ THEY ROT, BREED INSECTS AND DISEASES WHICH HARM TRUNK....

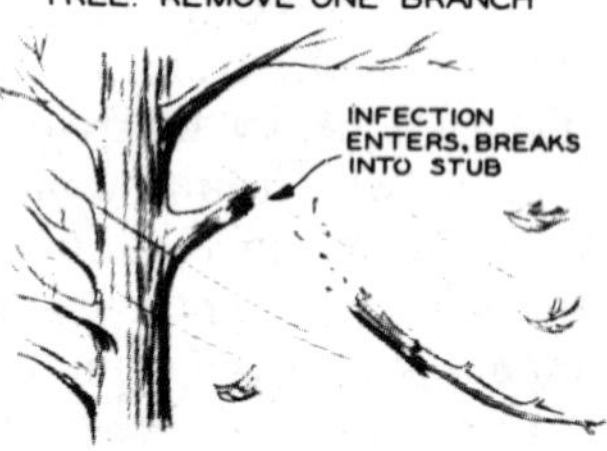

IF LEFT ALONE WINDS WILL SNAP OFF DEAD BRANCH ENDANGERING THOSE BELOW, AS WELL AS TRUNK

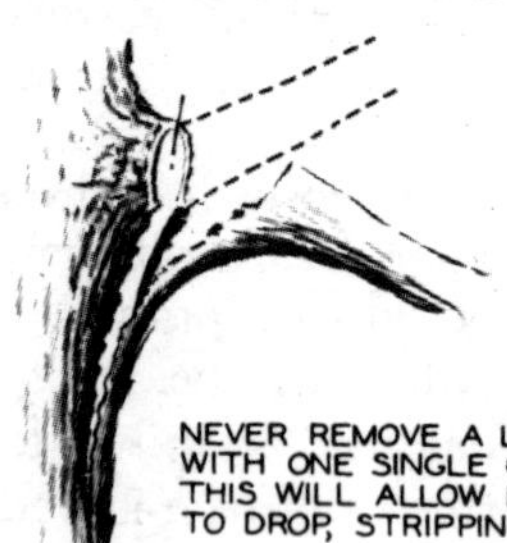

NEVER REMOVE A LIMB WITH ONE SINGLE CUT- THIS WILL ALLOW BRANCH TO DROP, STRIPPING BARK...

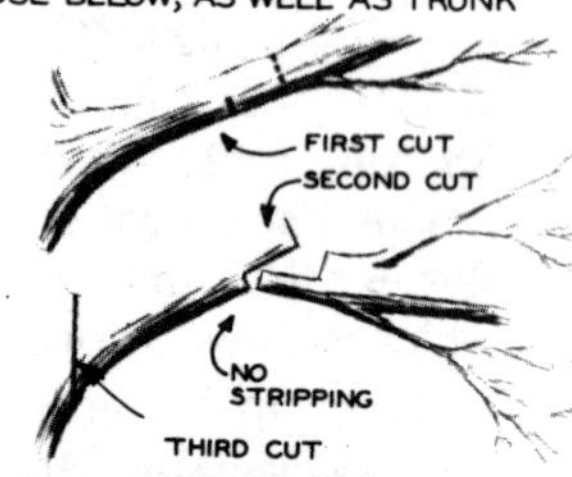

INSTEAD MAKE THREE SUCCESSIVE CUTS AS SHOWN ~ THIS GIVES CLOSE CLEAN CUT LEAVING NO VULNERABLE STUB

light and air to develop into strong flowering branches for the following season.

Pruning these immediately after blooming is ideal, but pressure of other work is great at that time so that it is often more practical to prune in fall, winter, or spring. This sacrifices some flowers but there is no great loss if the work is done intelligently. With some, forsythia for example, the prunings can be brought indoors and forced for winter bloom in vases of water.

If you prune shrubs that flower on old wood in winter or spring, cut out only weak and ill-placed branches and a few older branches to admit some light and air. Do not trim the ends off all the branches. Do not cut the shrubs hard back (unless you are purposely sacrificing a season's bloom to effect a complete rejuvenation). Just thin the bush somewhat.

Prune shrubs that flower on current season's wood in winter or early spring. Cut them back as far as you wish—almost to ground level if you want to keep the bushes as low as possible. Once the frame work of the bush is established at its required height, cut the previous year's growths back to within about one half inch of their bases. Thin out the weaker shoots that develop so that those retained are not crowded.

Most flowering trees and many deciduous shrubs need no considerable pruning every year. Magnolias, cherries, crab apples, dogwoods, azaleas, and gordonias for example.

Berried Shrubs. Do not prune shrubs grown for their ornamental fruits—barberries, viburnums, firethorns, etc. —more than absolutely necessary. Remove dead or badly placed branches and do a little judicious thinning out in early spring.

Evergreen Shrubs. Broad-leaved evergreens such as boxwood, mountain laurel, rhododendrons, azaleas, pieris, hollies, and barberries normally need no pruning other

NEVER LEAVE A BREAK OR CUT UNTREATED ~

APPLY WOUND DRESSING AFTER MAKING A CUT

AS TIME PASSES SAP WILL BUILD BARK OVER EDGES

ENTIRE FACE OF CUT WILL EVENTUALLY COVER COMPLETELY

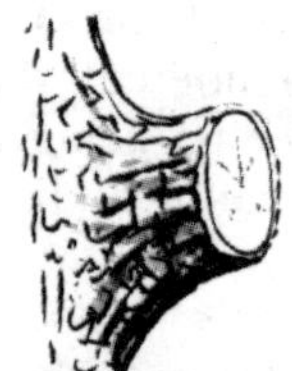

IF STUB IS ALLOWED TO REMAIN, OR NOT PROPERLY DRESSED ~

~ IT WILL DRY OUT, CRACK AND ALLOW INFECTION ~

LATER ROTTING THE TRUNK AND GUTTING TREE

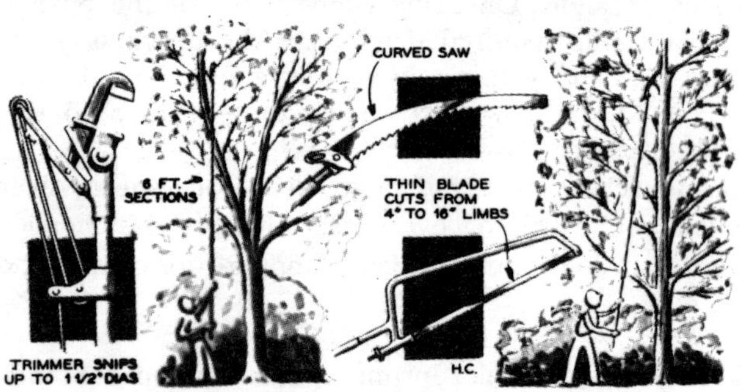

DO YOUR PRUNING FROM THE GROUND! SPECIAL TOOLS DESIGNED TO DO THE JOB OF SNIPPING TWIGS OR SAWING OFF THICK LIMBS ~ SECTIONAL POLES ARE THE ONLY PRACTICAL TREE REACHERS

that the shortening of an occasional over-ambitious branch. Yews may be kept compact by shortening their annual growths in summer or spring.

Vines. Evergreen vines should be pruned to keep them from becoming too dense or heavy, and to contain them within their allotted space. Prune just before new growth begins. Flowering vines should be pruned in spring if they bloom on current season's wood, immediately after flowering if they bloom on older wood. Summer pruning, which consists of shortening the young growths (when they become eighteen inches or so long) back to a length that includes only six or seven leaves from the base is greatly helpful in inducing wisterias to bloom. Cut the shortened growths back to a length of six inches in winter and to within half an inch of their bases after they flower (or, if they don't flower, after new leaf growth begins).

Roses. Climbing roses and species roses are pruned in summer immediately after they bloom, all others in spring just as growth begins.

Prune hybrid teas by cutting out all dead, weak, diseased, and crowded stems and by shortening back others to from four to eight inches. The rule is, the stronger the shoot the longer you leave it. Do the same with hybrid perpetuals but leave the shoots three or four times as long. Dwarf polyanthas and floribundas need little pruning other than cutting out of dead, diseased, and weak wood.

Climbing hybrid tea roses are pruned in spring or summer by removing an occasional old cane (provided new shoots are available to replace it) and by cutting off short, flowering shoots after the blooms have withered.

Prune climbers of the rambler and pillar types immediately after they bloom. Retain as many strong new canes as possible, and cut out as many old flowering growths as can be spared. With varieties that are free in producing new growths, prune out all the old, flowering wood. With those that produce but few new growths, it is often necessary to retain a few of the previous year's canes.

If you do this be sure to cut their side branches back close to the main cane.

Shrubby species roses are pruned by thinning them out after flowering.

Fruit Trees and Grape Vines. Prune fruit trees in late winter or early spring. Avoid summer pruning except with dwarf trees which should have their annual growths pinched back to six or seven leaves in July. Until fruit trees reach bearing age, prune lightly with the objective of developing a sound framework of well spaced branches. Cut out weak and interfering branches, and dead or diseased wood. Keep the centers of the trees fairly open to admit light and air, and to make pest control easier. Keep the trees moderate in height to facilitate spraying and harvesting. Avoid the development of sharp V crotches. Most bearing trees need annual pruning.

Apples and pears produce most of their fruit on older wood on short side growths called spurs. Prune these fruits by thinning out crowded shoots. Avoid excessive cutting back (except possibly when rejuvenating neglected trees). Never prune pears more than absolutely necessary. To do so encourages the dread fire blight disease.

Peaches and apricots need more pruning than other fruits. They bear along shoots produced the previous year. After the framework of the tree is formed, prune to force the production of strong, young growth each year. Cut out weak branches and twigs and cut back severely one third to one half of all the previous year's shoots that exceed a foot in length.

Cherries need no pruning other than corrective thinning once the framework is established. Pruning of established plums consists of judicious thinning to keep the top from becoming dense. No more of this should be done than absolutely necessary, however.

Roses

Two requirements above all others make for the successful cultivation of roses—plenty of sunshine and a deep, rich, well drained soil. With these you are far more than half way along the road to exhibition-quality flowers.

Once planted you expect roses to stay put for a long time. During those years you can add to the surface soil but you cannot directly modify the underlayers—where most of the roots are. Therefore, do the very best job possible before you plant. Make sure of good subsurface drainage. Condition the soil to a depth of two feet. Add plenty of humus, preferably in the form of half-rotted cow manure. Use bone meal liberally.

Soils on the heavy side are preferred to light sands or gravels. Don't interpret this to mean that infertile clays are suitable.

Roses need good air drainage. Low-lying pockets and places closed in by dense shrubbery or buildings provide conditions favorable to mildew and to their arch enemy, the black spot disease. Shelter from high, sweeping winds is desirable.

Ascertain which types and which varieties thrive best in your locality. There are tremendous differences in the adaptability of the particular roses. Get the best plants possible. Don't fall for bargain-priced offers by concerns not known to be thoroughly reliable. A good rose bush is a long time investment.

Selective disbudding–picking off buds to strengthen remaining ones–produces show blooms. Fading blossoms should be picked off regularly for tidiness' sake.

At right is a good rose bush before shipment from the nursery. The short cross lines show where the nurseryman will trim it before shipping. *Left:* Established hybrid tea properly pruned in the spring. Thicker canes of stronger varieties should not be pruned so far back. *Center:* This rose bush has been planted too deep.

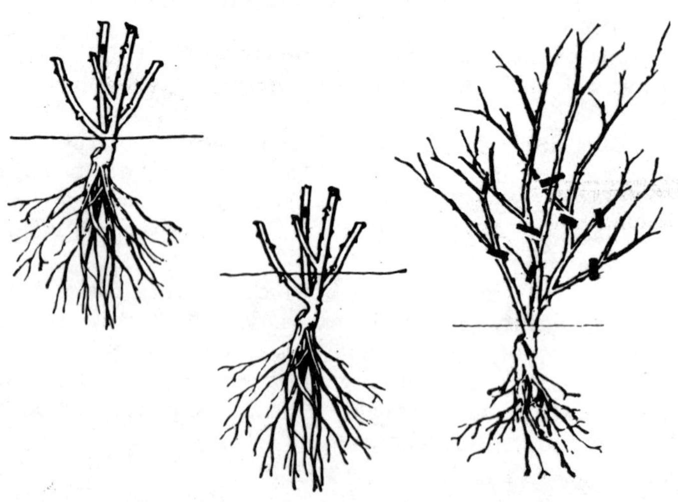

Plant in fall or early spring. Set budded or grafted plants (unless they are trained in tree form) so that the union of the bud or graft is just below the surface. Work good soil around the roots; pack it firmly.

If planted in the fall, prune moderately then severely the following spring. If spring-planted, prune hard at planting time.

Routine care of established roses consists of: (1) Pruning (see chapter "How to Prune"). (2) Fertilizing. A spring application of a complete fertilizer or of sheep manure, wood ashes, and bone meal cultivated into the surface followed by a dressing of complete fertilizer about midsummer is sufficient on fertile land. On poorer soils fertilize once a month but not later than August. (3) Watering. Never let roses suffer from lack of moisture. Soak the soil thoroughly at weekly intervals during dry weather. (4) Spraying and Dusting. You must persist with this if you want good roses. In early spring give a dormant spray of lime-sulphur. Keep the foliage covered with a fungicide throughout the entire summer. Watch for red spider and other insects. (5) Winter covering.

Irises

✤✤✤

The three most popular types of irises are bearded, Japanese, and Siberian. The bearded need sharp drainage and prefer neutral or slightly alkaline conditions. The Japanese and Siberian prefer slightly acid soils that are moist and rich in humus. They do not thrive if the ground is water-logged in winter.

If you have manure, use it heavily for Japanese and Siberian irises, more sparsely and not within three or four inches of the surface for the bearded. Lime may be used for the bearded; not for the others. All enjoy full sunshine.

Plant bearded kinds immediately after they bloom or in early fall after really hot weather is over, but while there is yet time for them to become established before winter. Plant Japanese and Siberian irises in early fall or in early spring. Lift and replant bearded and Japanese irises every third or fourth year, Siberians only as often as the clumps become so overcrowded that the flowers are sparse and weak.

When replanting, divide the bearded kinds so that each division consists of a single fan of leaves. Plant so that the top of the rhizome (root-like stem from which the leaves spring) is flush with the soil surface. Space the divisions nine inches to a foot apart.

Let each division of Japanese and Siberian irises con-

Japanese irises.

Bearded irises.

Dahlias.

Gladioli.

Peonies.

Delphinium.

sist of six or seven shoots. Plant about two feet apart and so that the crown or cluster of thin rhizomes is about two inches beneath the surface. At planting time cut back the foliage of all irises part way.

Bearded irises need little fertilizing. An annual application of bone meal and wood ashes is good. Big, old clumps of Siberians respond well to moderate fertilizing. Manure and bone meal or a complete, commercial fertilizer applied once a year is sufficient. Japanese irises are gross feeders. Manure them liberally. Fertilize them with a complete fertilizer in early spring, and again after they are through blooming.

Take care that the Japanese and Siberians have plenty of moisture from spring through fall. Water the bearded in times of drought. Keep dead flowers picked. In fall clean off and burn all dead and yellow foliage. In colder parts of the country mulch irises over winter with a very light covering of straw, salt hay, or evergreen branches. Under no circumstances use anything that will mat down and prevent air from circulating freely about the rhizomes. Bearded irises are subject to a rhizome rot disease. Remove all rotted rhizomes as soon as noticed, and disinfect soil and rhizomes with a special preparation intended for this purpose. Iris borers (worms that bore down in rhizomes) are troublesome. Spray with Sevin.

Peonies

With minimum care, peonies will live and bloom for more years than most garden plants. For ten, twenty-five or even fifty years undisturbed specimens may flower.

One secret is proper planting. The site should have sunshine for at least a half of each day. Full sun is better. The soil must be well drained.

Peonies root deeply. Prepare the ground to a minimum depth of a foot. Stock the soil with long-lasting fertilizer. If you use manure let it be old and rotted, and see that none is nearer than six inches to the surface. Supplement the manure with a pint of bone meal and twice as much unleached, wood ashes for each plant. If manure is not used, substitute compost, peat moss or leaf mold, and add a pint of organic, nitrogenous fertilizer. Mix the fertilizers thoroughly with the soil.

Dig holes for peony divisions at least eighteen inches in circumference. Plant as soon as you get the divisions from the nursery. Don't plant too deeply. Two inches of soil covering the crown of the plants is right.

Late summer or early fall is the best planting time, but plants can, if necessary, be moved late in fall or even in spring.

Every spring apply six ounces of complete fertilizer to each square yard, and cultivate it lightly into the soil.

Lifting, dividing, and replanting is usually desirable every five to ten years. Propagate by division in September. Each division should have four or more plump buds.

Dahlias

✣✣✣

Dahlias grow well if they get shade for part of each day; full sun is better. They like free air circulation but not sites exposed to strong winds. They are tolerant of a wide variety of soils; rich loam well supplied with humus suits them best.

Work the soil deeply. Enrich it with manure, bone meal and wood ashes or with a complete fertilizer.

Dahlias are frost-tender. Don't plant until settled, mild weather is assured. Set out either divisions of tubers or green plants. Green plants are raised from cuttings (or sometimes from seeds). Tubers may be planted ten days or two weeks earlier than green plants.

Space tall dahlias four feet apart each way, dwarfs, two to three feet. Drive stakes of proper height into place before planting.

For tubers dig holes six or seven inches deep and of ample width. Place the tuber on its side with its bud or eye pointed upwards. Carefully cover with soil until the hole is half filled. Complete the filling when the stem is a foot high.

Plant green plants in similar fashion leaving a hollow around each to be filled after the plants have made some growth. After planting water well, and shade for a few days if the weather is bright.

Stir the surface soil between dahlias repeatedly or mulch after the plants are growing well.

Allow only one shoot to each plant. When the first flower bud shows, pinch it out and, at the same time, pinch out the buds in the axils of the first two pairs of leaves immediately below that bud.

Let four to six of the lower side branches develop. Pinch out all side shoots that grow on these except the lowermost pair. When cutting the flowers, cut just above these retained shoots so that they, in turn, will develop and bear flowers.

Keep branches loosely tied to stakes.

Gladioli

Glads are tops among summer cut flowers. They are quickly grown and by planting successive batches you can have flowers from early summer to frost. For garden decoration they are lovely, too, but their uses for this purpose are limited because their individual spikes do not last long.

Glads need full sun. Any soil that will produce vegetables or that will support plantings of run-of-the-mill garden flowers is satisfactory. It must be well drained. Loosen it to a depth of from nine to twelve inches. Improve it with compost or similar organic matter. Fertilize it a couple of weeks before planting with a complete, vegetable garden fertilizer.

Make your first outdoor plantings as soon as danger of hard frosts is past. For early flowers, plant in cold-frames two or three weeks before this.

To insure a constant supply of flowers make successive plantings every two or three weeks until midsummer or later. The last planting should be made early enough to permit the flowers to develop before the killing frost. The number of growing days needed to do this varies with the variety, but ninety days may be taken as an average.

For cut flowers plant the corms (bulbs) in furrows, spacing those in each furrow either four inches apart in a single row or six inches apart in a double row. Let the furrows be four inches deep if the soil is heavy, an inch or two deeper in lighter soil. Cover the bulbs so that the soil surface is level, and firm the soil over them. Space the rows two to two-and-a-half feet apart. When planting in beds, place the corms six to eight inches apart. Plant with a trowel rather than with a dibble.

Like most bulbs, gladioli are sold according to size. Obtain those graded as number ones or number twos.

When the shoots are six inches high, pull soil up to a height of three or four inches against those planted in rows. Mulch the soil surface, or keep it regularly, but shallowly cultivated. When the second leaf is fully grown apply a complete, soluble fertilizer, and repeat this every two weeks until the buds show their petal color. Stake and tie, or provide other suitable supports to prevent the plants being damaged by storm.

Delphiniums

Delphiniums are technically perennials, but in most parts of America they are comparatively short lived and must be replaced from time to time. Few persist for more than four or five years.

Division, cuttings, and other vegetative means of propagation are rarely satisfactory. Fortunately, good results are obtainable from seeds with relative ease.

It is much better to raise your own than to buy ready-grown plants. Delphiniums do not ship well and few dealers offer plants as fine as those you can grow yourself with little trouble.

Get the best seeds available. Get them from a delphinium specialist. No matter how well you grow your plants, the flowers will be inferior if from a poor strain.

Sow the seeds in a light, well-drained soil to a depth of one eighth of an inch.

Seeds sown indoors in January or early February give plants which bloom outdoors in July and August. Those sown outdoors or in frames in April, late August, or September bloom the following year.

In cold climates keep plants raised from seeds sown in August or September in cold-frames over winter. Leave those from earlier sowing outdoors. Cover lightly with salt hay, straw, or evergreen branches.

Delphiniums need good drainage. They thrive best in

fertile loams but will grow in most soils that are not too clayey, provided they are nourishing. Do not use fresh manure. Well rotted manure is excellent. So is compost. Bone meal and wood ashes are excellent fertilizers, too. A neutral or slightly acid soil suits delphiniums best.

Set first year plants about two feet apart. In the second year re-space them to allow three or four feet between plants.

In early spring remove the winter covering. Apply six ounces of a 5-10-5 or the equivalent of another fertilizer to each square yard, and stir it lightly into the soil. Dust weekly with sulphur from the time the leaves unfold until the plants are in bud. Cut out weak or crowded stems. A year old plant should not retain more than five. Stake before the shoots are two feet tall. If the weather is dry, water copiously.

When the center spike has ceased blooming snip it out. Side branches will then flower. Snip those out too when their flowers fade. Don't cut the plants to the ground immediately after they have bloomed. Let them rest. When new shoots start, cut out the old growths and lightly till a dressing of fertilizer in the soil.

Cover very lightly in winter. Do not use peat moss, manure, or other material that is apt to lie wet for long periods.

Raising Young Plants Indoors

Even though you don't have a greenhouse you may want to start a few plants indoors so that you can be a jump ahead of the season. Tomatoes are favorites for this treatment; so are early cabbages, peppers, and eggplants. A number of flower garden annuals such as verbenas and snapdragons need an early start, and so do such flowering plants as cannas, tuberous begonias, geraniums, and begonias.

You have propagated these plants from seeds, cuttings, or divisions as described in the chapters in this book devoted to those subjects. But what about their after-care? What conditions and what attention do they need between the time they are successfully started as baby plants and the time they are ready to plant outside?

Well, I hope you didn't begin too early. That's a common fault. People get impatient. They start their plants indoors far too soon, with the result that they become overgrown, crowded, and weakly before planting-out time. It's better that the plants be a little backward rather than decidedly too far advanced at planting time.

The location where you grow your plants is important. Most need as much sunshine as possible and appreciate temperatures that at night are between 50 and 55 degrees. On dull days five degrees above night temperature is about right. When the sun is shining on the plants temperatures

10 or even 15 degrees higher than the night temperature is fine.

Keep the plants away from hot radiators and other sources of intense heat. Do not subject them to drafts, especially cold drafts. The idea that you must open windows because plants in the house "need fresh air" is nonsense. Ventilate only in mild weather. When it is really mild ventilate freely, particularly during the last week or so before the plants are moved outdoors. That is the time to "harden them off," to gradually accustom them to outdoor conditions.

Water young plants indoors with care. Once they have passed the very young, seedling stage, the trick is to thoroughly soak the soil each time the plants need water but to avoid wetting in between. No regular schedule can be set but avoid daily dribbles.

On bright, sunny days and especially on those breezy occasions which are good drying days, spray the foliage once or twice with water but don't wet the soil unless thorough watering is necessary. Never spray so late in the day that the foliage is moist at nightfall.

Newly propagated plants need transplanting to flats or individual pots before they become crowded and exhaust the soil. It is usual to set seedlings in flats, allowing about 2 inches between them, but sometimes they are moved to individual pots measuring 2½ inches in diameter.

Plants raised from cuttings are usually first potted into 2½-inch pots and may later be repotted into 3½- or 4-inch pots. Bulbous or tuberous plants such as tuberous begonias and cannas are most often started in 4-inch pots.

In all cases, use a loose, crumbly soil of moderate fertility. Good, fairly light topsoil mixed with equal parts peat moss (leaf mold or humus), and coarse sand with a pint of bone meal and a pint of sheep manure added to each bushel is about right.

Make sure the flats or pots are adequately drained. Have the new soil just moist, neither dry and dusty nor wet enough to stick to the fingers. Water the plants thoroughly a few hours before transplanting.

Handle the plants so that all possible roots are saved. Don't nip off the longest roots. Don't crowd them into a hole too small to hold them without bending or breaking and, of course, don't let them dry while they are out of the ground. Set seedlings that produce an opposite pair of first seed leaves (onions, lilies, and other monocotyledonous plants do not do this) with these leaves at ground level. Make the soil moderately firm, and water well immediately after the transplanting is done.

After transplanting, shade from direct sunshine for a few days, and sprinkle the foliage with water regularly (but not late in the day). Don't keep the soil saturated and do keep its surface lightly stirred and loosened with a pointed stick.

Some plants, snapdragons and petunias, for example, benefit if the tips of their main stems are nipped out to encourage branching.

One of the greatest difficulties you face when raising seedlings indoors are that they may "damp off" when tiny. Damping off means that the stems blacken and die at ground level with the result that the seedlings topple over and die. This is due to a fungus infection. But lack of sufficient light, temperatures that are too high, excessive wetness of the soil, and a too humid atmosphere favor the disease. Avoid these conditions and you have little to fear from damping off. Older plants do not ordinarily suffer from damping off but they will become leggy and spindly if they suffer from lack of light or high temperatures.

It's fun raising your own plants. A little patience, a lot of observation, and a good big dash of common sense will do much to turn the pinkest thumb a nice green hue. If you are uncertain of the color of yours, test it by trying to raise a few plants indoors.

How to Make Compost

Almost all soils need additional humus (the rare exceptions are woodland soils, and mucks that themselves largely consist of this material). In earlier times gardeners depended for humus very largely upon animal manures. These are now so scarce and expensive that few can obtain enough for their gardens.

Fortunately, the preparation of compost offers an easy and satisfactory method of meeting the deficiency either in whole or in part. Good compost is a most splendid form of humus. Prepare and use it.

Compost is made by decomposing organic matter (chiefly vegetable wastes, such as leaves and lawn clippings) in piles, bins or pits or by sheet composting on the ground surface.

The reasons for composting rather than burying the raw materials in the ground are (1) undecayed organic material buried in the soil in considerable quantities may make it temporarily less suitable for plant growth and (2) in garden practice the areas that need humus are very likely to be occupied by growing crops when the raw vegetation is available.

Organic wastes are changed into compost by bacteria, fungi, protozoa, and other microscopic or minute organisms and by the activities of some larger creatures such as earthworms.

In order to work effectively they need (1) moisture in reasonable amounts, for if the material is too dry or is saturated, loss of efficiency results. (2) Oxygen. Decomposition does not take place at a satisfactory rate unless air permeates the vegetable waste. (3) A suitable temperature. The temperature maintained is partly dependent upon fermentation of the waste materials and partly upon atmospheric temperature. In warm weather decay proceeds more quickly than in cold.

Dozens of different systems of making compost have been advocated. All depend for success upon the same principles. For the best and quickest results keep together plant wastes that decay at about the same rate. Do not put woody branches of trees and shrubs along with softer, more easily decayable materials. If possible, build sizable heaps so that interior heat will be conserved and a comparatively high temperature maintained. Add a moderate amount of an organism-containing activator such as manure, decayed compost, rich garden soil or special cultures of micro-organisms that are offered commercially. This gives the heap a start. The principle is the same as that of adding yeast to bread dough. Add nutrients, particularly nitrogen and phosphorous. Add lime to counteract acidity.

So much for the principles involved. How shall you go about making your own compost pile? Collect all plant residues except those of a definitely woody character. You will have, perhaps, weeds, lawn mowings, tree leaves, non-woody prunings, remains of annuals, perennials and vegetables, old hay, straw and kitchen wastes such as grapefruit and banana skins—it's simply amazing how much accumulates in a season in even a small garden. Don't put in the general compost heap sawdust, shavings, pine needles or leaves of evergreens. Unless specially treated these do not decay satisfactorily.

Animal residues, such as fish-heads and chicken innards, theoretically make good compost but if you add them to the heap they are apt to attract the neighborhood dogs and cats as well as more undesirables such as rats. Better bury them deeply or dispose of them in some other way.

As a safety measure I do not recommend using material that is infected with such soil-borne diseases and pests as crown rot of delphinium and the chrysanthemum nematode, although if the temperature inside the heap rises to 140 degrees or more (and it should) and if the outsides of the heap are turned to the interior while the heap is hot there should be no danger.

There is no objection to composting plants affected with wind-borne diseases such as mildew, black-spot, and rust or with such insects as plant lice, red spider mites and mealy bugs. These should all be killed in the composting process but if a few escape they are no more threatening than those which will come in from above-ground sources anyway.

The compost pile works best when it is protected from winds which reduce its temperature and dry it and from direct sun which also has a drying effect. A sheltered location in the shade is desirable. A width of four to eight feet is suitable. It can be of any length. Begin by spreading a couple of inches of manure, old compost or fertile soil on the bottom. Add your vegetable wastes as they accumulate.

Every time the added material becomes six inches deep sprinkle it with a complete garden fertilizer (4 to 6 ounces to a square yard is about enough) and an equal amount of ground limestone (or a slightly less amount of agricultural lime). Moisten the material if it is at all dry (but don't saturate it) and then cover with a quarter inch layer of good soil. Then begin adding more waste and so on until the heap is four or five feet high. Let the sides slope slightly inward and make the top slightly hollow.

You may substitute tankage, dried blood, sheep manure or farmyard manure and some superphosphate or bone meal for the commercial fertilizer recommended above. The purpose is to add nitrogen and phosphorus.

NATURAL ORGANIC FERTILIZERS	Percentage of Available Nitrogen	Percentage of Phosphoric Acid	Percentage of Potash	Speed of Availability to the Plant	Amount in pounds per hundred square feet for an Average Application
Horn shavings	15	a little		slow	3 lbs
Dried blood	8-14	a little	a little	fairly rapid	3 lbs
Tankage	9-11	a little	a little	rather slow	5 lbs
Fish meal	7-10	4-8		rather slow	3 lbs
Cottonseed meal	6-9	2-3	1½-2	rather slow	3 lbs
Activated sludge (Milorganite)	6	2½		fairly rapid	3 lbs
Dried poultry manure	5-6	2-3	1-2	fairly rapid	5 lbs
Bone-meal	2-4	20-25		slow	5 lbs
Tobacco stems	2-3		4-10	rather slow	5 lbs
Dried cattle manure	1-2	1-2	2-3	rather slow	5 lbs
Pulverized sheep manure	1-2	1-2	2-3	fairly rapid	5 lbs
INORGANIC AND SYNTHETIC FERTILIZERS					
Ureaform fertilizers	46			slow	½ lb
Sulphate of ammonia	20			rapid	1 lb
Nitrate of soda	15			very rapid	1½ lbs
Muriate of potash			48-50	rapid	1 lb
Sulphate of potash			48-50	rapid	1 lb
Superphosphate 20%		20		rather slow	5 lbs
Treble superphosphate 45%		45		rather slow	2 lbs
Nitrate of potash	14		45	very rapid	1 lb

After a few weeks the inside of the heap will be half decayed (the time needed for this to occur depends upon the temperature, character of the material, and other variables). When this stage is reached, turn the heap in such a way that the undecayed outsides become the insides of the new pile. If it is dry moisten it somewhat but don't saturate it. When the material has decayed to the extent that it is a black or dark brown spongy mass and no structure of leaf or stems is visible, its processing is complete.

Sheet composting—breaking up and churning fresh organic matter into the upper three or four inches of soil (where air is available in sufficient quantities) saves the labor of transporting materials and of turning the piles.

Some Plants Need Support

Staking and tying are among the least understood garden arts. Master them if you want your garden to have that well-finished look that only orderliness and neatness can give.

Good staking pays off not only in improved appearance but also by preserving your flowers and plants. Tomato fruits are cleaner and less liable to rot if they are raised above the ground on suitable supports; the staked gladiolus develops into a fine, usable cut flower rather than the crooked-stemmed example it may produce if unsupported; the delphinium is protected from storm breakage, newly planted trees are secured until roots take hold.

Good staking means that each plant is adequately supported, that the supports are placed in position early, that no more supports than necessary are used, that they are suited to the kinds of plants, and that they are as inconspicuous as possible.

Not only should stakes be inconspicuous, but so should the effects of staking. Stems should not be bunched together in unnatural positions. Plants should seem to have grown as they are.

As supports, numerous devices are used varying from arbors and trellises to bean poles, slender bamboos, and strings. The former are most useful for woody plants that do not die down over winter, such as climbing roses, grapevines, and wisterias. When trellises for such plants are built against wooden houses, hinge them near their bases so that they can be leaned outwards from the house at painting time. Make supports for heavy vines, such as wisterias, sturdy enough to serve well when the vines are fully grown.

Choose rot-resistant woods such as locust, cedar, redwood, and cypress for plant supports. Do not creosote them. Asphalt paint and wood preservatives based on copper may be used on the parts that go underground. Charring the lower ends of stakes from their bases to an inch or two above the soil line is excellent.

Wire and other metal supports are advantageous for some plants, grapes, raspberries, and wisterias, for example. The chief fault is that they become so hot in sunshine, they may burn tender shoots. This is not troublesome with the plants mentioned because their leaves shade the wires early in the season. With plants that renew themselves from the ground each year the ill effects can be more serious.

Wooden stakes, round or square, varying in length from five to eight feet, and in thickness from one to one-and-a-half inches, are excellent for dahlias, tomatoes, and other heavy growers. Paint them almost black-green. Bamboo canes of various thicknesses, ranging in length from two to six feet, are useful for a wide variety of perennials, lilies, gladioli, and annuals. They may be had in natural color or painted green.

Stakes from two to six feet tall, made from No. 8 or No. 10 gauge wire, each with an open loop or a loose spiral at the top, are excellent for a wide variety of plants, particularly those of frail, slender growth.

Tall, tapering poles formed of sapling trees are suitable for climbing beans. Leave short stubs where the side branches were, rather than cutting them flush.

Brushwood, particularly twiggy brushwood such as that of wild cherry, makes excellent support not only for peas and sweet peas, but also for many annuals and perennials. Chicken wire of three-quarter-inch mesh is commonly used and is satisfactory for peas and sweet peas that are grown in rows.

Put stakes in position before stems are crooked or damaged. In the case of beans, nasturtiums, morning glories, and other annual vines do this before the seeds are sown and for dahlias, tomatoes, and the like, before the plants are set out. Place brushwood to peas shortly after they appear above ground.

To stake well you must have a knowledge of the habits of growth and the heights that the plants attain. Brushwood, which is excellent for such subjects as chrysanthemums, should be pushed between the plants before they are half grown. The stems then grow up through the interlacing branches of the brush and no tying is needed. Before the plants bloom, cut off protruding tips of brush. Sharpen the ends of the brushwood stakes and push them deeply into the ground.

Four or five really tall pieces of brushwood with their bases forming a circle and their tops tied together to form a pyramid or tepee give good support to groups of annual vines planted around them.

Always push stakes deeply into the ground. Don't set them in too close to the stems of lilies and other bulbous plants or you may drive them through the bulbs and cause serious injury.

Use soft string or raffia for tying. Twist the tie around the stake a point higher than that at which it goes around the stem. Twist the strings a couple of times between the stake and the stem to make them one, as it were, rather than two separate strings. Always tie square knots rather than "grannies"—which pull open and release the ties under a little strain. Tie against the plant stem rather than against the stake. Allow necessary room for growth. Don't tie too tightly. On the other hand don't tie so loosely that the stems can be injured by whipping about in winds.

Often you can tie several stems to one stake. If you do don't bunch them together like sheaves of wheat. Tie them more or less individually so that they are gracefully and naturally disposed.

Your Garden Calendar

JANUARY • New catalogs from seedsmen and nurserymen are now available. Study them carefully. Make out orders for what you need. Stick chiefly to varieties that have proven themselves, but be venturesome enough to try a few of the season's novelties, even though in modest amounts only.

Do you have enough flats and pots to meet your spring requirements? If not, order these. Consider also the matter of tools, and place orders for any you need, but only those of workmanlike design, of good quality, and suited to the strength of the user. Poor tools are a poor investment.

If you intend to sow seeds early indoors, check that you have "the makings" for the soil mixtures you will need—topsoil, coarse sand, and humus or peat moss under cover. You'll need them fairly dry, free of frost, and in a hurry when sowing time arrives.

Keep an eye on evergreens. Shake or brush them off to prevent accumulations of snow. Do this while the snow is dry and powdery, before it becomes wet and heavy enough to break branches. A wooden rake is a good implement to use for the purpose. Christmas tree branches make good winter protection for low evergreens and for perennials that keep their leaves through the winter. Use those from your own tree as well as any others you can get.

Periodically check the bulbs in storage—dahlias, gladioli, tuberous begonias, etc. Remove any that are decaying. See that they are not kept where they are so hot and dry that they shrivel, or so warm and moist that they begin to grow.

In the South, prepare soil for spring planting just as soon as it is in condition to work. Cut back severely the shrubs which may be in need of this treatment because they have grown too tall and leggy. In the lower South, sowing of the hardier vegetables such as lettuce, carrots, spinach, and radish, and of hardy annuals can now be made. Also plant gladioli for early blooms. Thin seedlings of fall-sown annuals before they crowd each other.

Biennials and young perennials in cold-frames are dormant now. Do not let temperatures inside the frames become too high on sunny days. Ventilate the frames as soon as the frost on the glass begins to melt. Snow is a good natural protection. Do not brush it off the glass.

FEBRUARY • Make sure that evergreens in very exposed positions are shielded from strong sunshine and sweeping winds by burlap screens, evergreen branches or other means. This month and the next are extremely difficult for evergreens. Don't worry if the leaves of rhododendrons curl into tight pencils in really cold weather. This is natural. It conserves moisture in the plant tissues. During mild weather, water very thoroughly the evergreens planted under overhanging roofs or elsewhere where they do not receive ample rainfall.

Cut and bring inside budded branches of forsythia, flowering peach, flowering almond, apple, and pussywillow for forcing into bloom in water. These will soon bloom in a sunny window. Cut them if possible during mild, moist weather. Force also branches of birch, horsechestnut, and other trees. Even though they do not flower they will soon develop some of the finest greenery imaginable—a real foretaste of spring.

Watch perennials carefully. Thaws and rains may form puddles which drown the plants or which freeze over and exclude air. You can often prevent damage by opening up miniature ditches with a hoe to drain away the superfluous water. During thaws, push into place any plants that have heaved. See that material used for winter covering does not pack down tightly over the plants.

Sow seeds of annuals indoors that need a long season of growth, such as vincas lobelias, begonias and snapdragons, also such perennials as delphiniums and coreopsis that bloom the first year from seed.

Inspect trees and shrubs closely for egg clusters of tent caterpillars and other injurious insects, and also for cocoons. A little time spent collecting and destroying them now will save much of the effort needed to eradicate them later.

Collect and store all ashes from your wood burning fireplace in a dry place for future use. They are a valuable fertilizer—a grand source of potash.

In the South, plant trees, shrubs, and roses. Plant gladioli as soon as danger of severe frost has passed. Apply dormant sprays to control scale insects. Do this only when the temperature is forty degrees or more. Divide and transplant perennials. Sow annuals and early vegetables.

In California, take cuttings of carnations to bloom in December. Prune poinsettias severely. Attend to the necessary pruning of winter-blooming shrubs immediately after they stop blooming. After pruning, fertilize or apply a nourishing mulch to the ground.

MARCH • Don't take covering off too early. It's no use exposing plants unnecessarily to the last biting blasts of winter. Uncover gradually. If possible, choose dull, moist, weather for the job. Sow hardy vegetables and annuals as soon as the ground is workable. In New York, peas and such hardy flowers as cornflowers, larkspurs, poppies, and sweet peas may be planted around the middle of the month.

Finish all spring pruning including that of hybrid tea, and hybrid perpetual roses. Apply dormant sprays to control scale insects and some other pests and diseases. Use the 'sprays before the buds burst. Don't let lime-sulphur drift on to painted surfaces. It stains them badly. Don't use dormant sprays when the temperature is below forty degrees or is likely to drop to freezing point during the night following their use.

If digging was not completed in the fall, get busy as soon as the ground is workable. This will be earlier on plots where winter rye was sown as a cover crop than on bare ground. Sweep the lawn. Top dress it or fertilize it and re-seed bare patches as soon as possible. Don't roll it until it has dried out sufficiently so that this will not pack the soil too hard.

Sow seeds of most annuals that are to be raised indoors for planting out later. Six to eight weeks is enough for most kinds to reach planting-out size. Calculate sowing dates accordingly. Make sowings of early vegetables—cabbages, cauliflowers, broccoli, lettuce, celery, tomatoes, peppers, etc., indoors. Also start tuberous-rooted begonias and cannas indoors so that you will have good plants to set out in May.

Harden biennials and other plants that have been wintered in cold-frames in readiness for planting them outdoors. Get the hotbed started.

In the South plant or sow tender vegetables such as beans, tomatoes, corn, and squash as soon as the ground is warm and frost danger is passed. Plant gladioli, dahlias, cannas, tuberoses, and other summer bulbs. Keep rye grass planted to provide winter lawns closely cut to keep it from harming the permanent lawn grasses. Repair bare patches on the lawn. Don't let lawns or other parts of the garden suffer from lack of water.

On the West Coast turn under fall cover crops. As weather permits, sow hardy vegetables outdoors, the more tender ones in frames. Apply cutworm and slug baits to the soil before planting.

APRIL • Push on as rapidly as possible with spading and other ground work. Plant evergreens, trees, shrubs, vines, roses, and perennials. When weather permits set out pansies, English daisies and other biennials from the cold-frames. Choose cloudy, still days for this work.

If you must sow your new lawn in spring rather than fall do so without delay. Roll the established lawns, choosing a time when the soil is fairly dry. If you have not fertilized the lawn yet, do so. Dig out dandelions and other weeds.

Fertilize perennial beds and lightly fork them over. Take care not to damage shoots of balloon flowers and other late appearers that are not yet above ground. Keep the young foliage of peonies sprayed regularly with Bordeaux mixture to check botrytis. Keep hollyhocks dusted with sulphur. Don't cut down foliage of bulbs until it has turned completely brown. When cutting flowers of daffodils and other bulbs take no more foliage than absolutely necessary. All bulbs benefit from a dressing of complete fertilizer applied before they are half-grown.

After danger of hard frost is past, plant early gladioli. For succession make later plantings at two-week intervals. Sow all kinds of hardy annuals and all vegetables except those that are frost-tender. Don't make the common mistake of sowing at one time too much of any one vegetable. Successive sowings of modest amounts are the thing.

In the South keep roses dusted or sprayed regularly. Disbud roses if you want the finest cut flowers. Plant tender vegetables as soon as all danger from frost has passed. Sow seeds of heat-resistant annuals such as zinnias, cosmos, marigolds, sunflowers, petunias and morning glories. Plant cannas, dahlias, gladioli, and tuberoses.

As soon as their blooming is finished, prune shrubs that benefit from this attention. Bermuda grass lawns can be made now either by seeding or sodding.

In West Coast gardens spray citrus trees to control scale. Make successive plantings of vegetables. Don't let the garden suffer from dryness. Make particularly sure that azaleas, camellias, and other plants in active growth receive ample amounts of moisture. Mulch roses and other plants.

Seeds of most summer flowering annuals can be sown.

Sow seeds of Gerbera in California gardens as soon as the soil is warm.

MAY • Give attention this month to setting out frost-tender plants. In the vegetable garden sow corn, beans, squash, and cucumbers, in the flower garden set out zinnias, marigolds, morning glories, nasturtiums, four o'clocks, etc. Plant bulbs of dahlias, montbretias, begonias, and tuberoses.

Plants which have been raised indoors and hardened are now ready for setting in the garden. First, put out the hardier kinds such as cabbage, cauliflower, broccoli, celery, snapdragons, stocks, asters, petunias. As the weather warms, follow with egg-plants, peppers, tomatoes, lantanas, geraniums, heliotropes, and fuchsias. Don't make the mistake of setting out the more tender kinds too early. Nothing is gained. Wait until the weather is really settled.

Disturbing dry spells may occur in May. Give plenty of water when watering is necessary. Do not let newly set out plants suffer from dryness. Be sure that bulbs do not lack moisture during the entire time that their foliage is green. After their foliage has completely browned, remove it and lift the bulbs for summer storage, or leave them in place and plant annuals over them if you prefer to do this. Keep the cultivator busy among young plants. Nothing promotes growth and discourages weeds better than frequent surface cultivation. A warning must be sounded, however, against hoeing among shrubs that root right at the surface, as do rhododendrons and azaleas.

Pick dead flowers off lilacs as they fade. Seed production is an exhausting process. Make sure that supports for peonies and other plants are in place early. Put supports for pole beans, tomatoes, and other annual crops in position before you sow or plant. Disbud peonies and roses if you wish the finest flowers for cutting. This is not important if the plants are for garden decoration only. Towards the end of the month sow seeds of dephiniums, coreopsis, painted daisies, and other perennials in a cold-frame or sheltered outdoor bed.

In the South sow okra, watermelons, cantaloupes, and beans of various kinds. Set eggplants, peppers and sweet potatoes. Make a second sowing of vegetable seeds to produce late crops. For mid-season bloom sow balsams, cockscombs, cosmos, globe amaranth, moonflower, torenias, and zinnias.

Maintain a steady warfare against pests and diseases, keep the surface soil repeatedly cultivated or else mulch it. Water freely in dry weather.

In Western gardens sow and plant the more tender crops. Provide irrigation as this is necessary. Sow all kinds of annuals.

JUNE • You may still plant dahlias. Set out tropical waterlilies now. Continue to make sowings of vegetables and annuals for succession. Sow seeds of most biennials—foxgloves, forget-me-nots, sweet-williams, Siberian wallflowers and the like. Pinch the tips out of chrysanthemum shoots each time they make six inches of growth.

Don't cut peony blooms too low. Always leave ample foliage on the parts of the stems left with the plant. Portulaca may be common but it's wonderful for covering spaces where spring bulbs have been. Just broadcast the seed. Portulaca must have full sun.

Apply mulches to keep down weeds. Where these are not used stir the soil frequently and shallowly with the hoe. Good work with the H-O-E-S saves need for the H-O-S-E. Remember surface cultivation conserves the soil moisture. Don't prolong the asparagus cutting season. To do so weakens the plants. Shear back candytuft, basket-of-gold, pink daphne, pinks, and many other rock garden and border plants of low stature immediately after they bloom. Dust roses regularly to keep down black spot. Attend to other needed pest and disease control measures. If irises are to be replanted after they have bloomed, do not delay. Be sure to cut out all diseased parts and destroy pesky borers. The best way with hollyhocks is to destroy them after they have flowered and raise new ones each year from June-sown seed. These are much less liable to rust disease than are old plants. As soon as the June drop (natural falling off) of such fruits as peaches and apricots is completed, thin the fruits to whatever degree is needed. Plant gladioli bulbs all through this month. Avoid letting the annual shoots of wisterias get long and twisted together. Cut them back to just above the sixth or seventh leaf from the base. Staking and tying needs frequent attention. As soon as polyanthus primroses have finished blooming, divide and reset them in a fairly moist soil containing humus. They should be placed in a lightly shaded place. Many small, rock-garden plants which make active new growth after flowering may be treated likewise.

In the South feed camellias and azaleas. Don't hoe near these shrubs. They are surface rooters. Prune climbing roses. Trim edges of Bermuda grass lawns to prevent the grass invading cultivated beds.

In West Coast gardens carry on warfare against slugs. In California sow delphinium seeds. Cut back snapdragons and other flowers that respond to this treatment to encourage second blooming.

JULY • Cultivate frequently but not deeply. Deep cultivation between growing plants harms them by destroying feeding roots near the surface. Draw earth around the bases of corn to prevent the stalks being blown down. Sow beets, carrots, and rutabagas for winter storage. Set out plants of cabbage, cauliflower, kale, and broccoli for late crops. Towards the latter part of the month sow head lettuce, radishes, and turnips.

Don't mow the lawn too closely. Set the mower to cut at a height of two inches. In dry spells water the grass thoroughly at about weekly intervals. Daily sprinklings are worse than useless. Don't fertilize the lawn at this time but do feed roses, dahlias, gladioli, and vegetables with soluble fertilizers.

Keep faded flowers picked or cut from snapdragons, phlox, lupines, delphiniums, and other plants. This encourages them to keep blooming. Cut back lightly and fertilize alyssum, petunias, verbenas, and other annuals that are a little straggly and weary looking. This will give them a new lease on life. As soon as rambler roses have finished blooming cut out at ground level all old flowering canes that can be spared and tie in new shoots that spring from the base. A mulch of rotted manure with some bone meal added or a light dressing of commercial fertilizer applied now benefits both climbing and bush roses. Cut out fruiting canes of raspberries as soon as the fruit has been gathered. This applies to the everbearing kinds as well as the others.

Don't permit seed pods to form on rhododendrons. Pick off the flower clusters when faded. If at all possible, mulch all evergreens, particularly broad-leaved kinds. Shear evergreen hedges now—those of hemlock, yew, and aborvitae, for instance. Keep a keen look-out for the pesky red spider mite on hemlocks, spruces, phlox, primroses, and other plants. Dusting with sulphur gives good control, but don't do this if the temperature is ninety degrees or above. Watch for lace bugs on the undersides of the leaves of azaleas, rhododendrons, and cotoneaster. To prevent, spray with nicotine. Lift, transplant, and divide narcissi that are crowded.

In Southern gardens plant tomatoes for the fall crop. Cut back the tips of poinsettias if you do not want them to grow too tall. Don't let nandinas get really dry or they may drop their berries.

On the West Coast propagate camellias, heathers, and other choice evergreens from cuttings.

AUGUST • This is the time to divide and replant oriental poppies. Madonna lilies may also be lifted, divided, and replanted. Plant colchicum bulbs. Study bulb catalogs and place orders for fall requirements early. Narcissi and daffodils in particular should be obtained as early as the dealer can supply them. Plant them as soon as possible after you receive them. Order perennials you want for fall planting as well as trees, shrubs, roses, and evergreens.

Evergreen planting may be begun during the last part of this month. Prune French hydrangeas by cutting out close to their bases all old, flowering shoots as the flowers fade. Don't cut the strong, new non-flowering shoots that are developing. These should bloom next year.

If you plan to sow a new lawn next month (the best time of the year) begin getting the ground in condition without delay. By grading and conditioning it early you give annual weeds a chance to grow and yourself an opportunity to hoe them down and thus produce a fairly weed-free seed bed before you sow your grass.

Sow winter rye or rye grass on areas of the vegetable and cut-flower garden that become vacant. These cover crops provide valuable humus when they later are turned into the soil. Collect herbs for drying about the time their first flowers open. If they are at all mud-splashed, wash them in running water before drying them. The white, dusty coating that appears on phlox, lilac, rose, and other leaves in late summer is mildew. It can be prevented by dusting with sulphur.

Keep a garden notebook. It's important at all times, but never more so than now when the results of your efforts are plainly before you. Next year's garden should be based on this year's notes.

In the South, sow fall vegetbles including cabbage, Chinese cabbage, rutabagas, mustard, collards, carrots, snap beans, onions, and radishes. Sow flower garden annuals too—balsams, marigolds, zinnias, cosmos, and petunias among others. Keep faded flower heads off crepe myrtles. Do not push roses by feeding or watering them this month. Allow them to rest awhile. Hand-pick bagworms on junipers and arborvitae, or destroy them by spraying with Sevin.

In West Coast gardens sow annuals for winter blooming such as calendulas, cinerarias, nemesias, phlox, calecolarias, alyssum candytuft, and winter blooming sweet peas. In California plant ranunculus, callas, freezias, and other winter-flowering bulbs. Divide and replant clivias.

SEPTEMBER • Sow lawns this month. The cool weather of fall with the ground yet warm and moist gives grasses the best possible chance for development. Renovation of old lawns by weeding, top dressing, fertilizing, and reseeding is also in order.

Evergreen planting should be in full swing now. If the weather is at all dry, water newly set evergreens copiously and soak established evergreens periodically. They will survive the winter much more surely if they are not subjected to extreme dryness during the fall. Plant new peonies this month and divide and replant any that need this treatment. Continue to plant winter rye on vacant land. Give hedges their last searing now.

Make cuttings of tender perennials you wish to winter indoors. Among these may be geraniums, ageratums, fuchsias, heliotropes, coleus, blood-leaf, begonias, and abutilons. Get all plants that need protection under cover before frost comes. If you lift plants such as geraniums and begonias from beds or window boxes and plant them in pots to keep them over winter, use well-drained pots and light, sandy soil. Cut the plants back about half way and keep them shaded and in a moist atmosphere (such as that of a closed cold-frame) for a week or two until their roots reestablish themselves.

Lift and store dahlias, gladioli, tuberous begonias, tiger flowers, montbretias, tuberoses, and other tender bulbs after their foilage has been frosted. Gather all waste vegetation and build it into a compost heap.

In dull weather transplant to their flowering locations hardy chrysanthemums that have been grown in a reserve border. If carefully moved with a ball of soil, these plants can be shifted from place to place without any unfavorable results.

In the South sow for spring blooming coreopsis, bluebonnets, larkspurs, annual phlox, cornflowers and, where they are hardy, snapdragons, calendulas, stocks, and petunias. Sow beets, carrots, lettuce, and other vegetables. Sow winter lawns of Italian rye grass.

In West Coast gardens watch out for slug damage.

Renovate California lawns now. Rake out Bermuda grass, fertilize, and sow lawn grass seed. Keep ground moist. Sow all kinds of annuals and vegetables now. Continue to plant winter flowering bulbs, those mentioned in last month's calendar as well as anemones, lachenalias, watsonias, and brodieas.

OCTOBER • Don't burn leaves. Collect all you can from deciduous trees and shrubs and stack them for compost, omit from the compost heap leaves of evergreens, though. Gather other nonwoody plant refuse, including weeds, and put it on the compost pile (except material that may carry soil-borne disease). Plant almost all deciduous trees, shrubs, fruits, vines, and roses. Do this sufficiently early for their roots to have a chance to take hold before growth activity ceases. Plant perennials. This is a grand month in which to re-make the perennial border, and it needs re-making every three or four years. Do the best possible job of soil improvement before you replant. Heel in the plants you lift from the border while soil improvement is in progress.

Plant all kinds of spring-blooming bulbs. Most are better if set in the ground as early as possible but with tulips it is advisable to wait fairly late—until early November in the vicinity of New York City. Dig up and pot parsley and chives for growing indoors to supply winter "greens." Don't let leaves accumulate on the lawn. Continue to cut the grass as long as it grows but don't cut it shorter than two inches. There is still time to plant winter rye as a cover crop. This is especially valuable on slopes. It prevents erosion. It also adds considerable humus to the soil when it is turned up come spring.

Clean up the garden. Pull and burn iris and peony leaves when they are thoroughly brown and dry. This is a sanitation measure. Make sure that legible labels are attached to all plants in which you have a special interest. It's so easy to forget names, and insecure labels are easily lost in winter.

Exposure to winter frosts is of special value in conditioning heavy, clayey soils. If yours is of this type, spade under manure or rough compost and leave the surface in large clods. If last month's frost did not blacken dahlias and other plants that are stored over winter it probably will this month. Lift and get these plants under cover as soon as this occurs.

In the South order fruit trees for November and December planting. Dig sweet potatoes before the frost. Plant bulbs. Sow early-flowering sweet peas and other annuals. Sow beets, carrots, collards, lettuce, onions, radishes, and turnips. You can still sow winter lawns of rye grass.

On the West Coast plant bulbs in great variety including watsonias, anemones, freesias, montbretias, and ranunculus. Renovate lawns. Sow seeds of native wild flowers.

NOVEMBER • Make sure that newly planted trees are securely staked or guyed. Winter storms will test them. Plant tulip bulbs before the ground freezes hard. Keep evergreens well watered until really hard freezing weather arrives. Mulch newly planted trees, shrubs, evergreens, and perennials early so that the soil is kept warm enough to encourage root activity longer than would otherwise be the case. Perennials that are slightly tender, as chrysanthemums are in some localities, may be wintered-over successfully in cold-frames. Plant them in sandy, well-drained soil. Secure collars of quarter-inch wire mesh or light roofing paper around fruit and other trees liable to be gnawed or chewed by rabbits and mice. Let these collars extend at least two inches into the ground and two feet above it. It is a good plan to wrap the trunks of newly transplanted trees tightly in burlap. This prevents the bark from splitting as a result of exposure to winter sunshine and consequent alternate freezing and thawing. It is also effective in denying borers entrance to the trunks.

Roses may be planted now. Just before the ground freezes, mound them up with soil. If you have ordered lilies or other bulbs that have not yet arrived, mulch the planting sites heavily to keep out frost, then, when the bulbs finally come, you can plant them without difficulty. Do not apply protective winter mulches to established plants until the soil is frozen at least two inches deep. Newly set plants may be mulched earlier. Turn over the compost pile for the final time this year. This will speed its even decomposition.

Complete cleaning up. Cut all perennials down close to ground level. Continue spading as late as possible. There is much more time now than in spring for ground work. This goes for new construction projects too—rock-garden building, for example.

In the South continue to plant vegetables and annuals. Divide and replant perennials. Among the most satisfactory are shasta daisy, coreopsis, sweet violet, gaillardia, moss pink, physostegia, beebalm, and perennial asters. Plant spring-flowering bulbs. Transplant trees and shrubs.

In the West plant artichokes. Sow sweet peas. Sow seeds of native wild flowers. Plant figs, oranges, lemons, and also roses. In all cases do as good a job as possible of soil preparation. This is the foundation of success in all gardening.

DECEMBER • Corn stalks may harbor the European corn-borer. Don't leave them lying around. Burn them, or better still, bury them a foot or more underground. There they will decay to form humus, and the borers will die. Before really severe cold weather arrives cover the strawberry bed with straw or other loose mulch material to a depth of three or four inches. Examine raspberry canes and cut out and burn swollen sections that are caused by insect activity. Apply winter covering to perennials, biennials, and rock-garden plantings. Do not put this on too heavily. A two or three inch layer is ample. It is important not to use dense mulches such as peat moss on plants that retain their leaves through the winter. For these, salt hay, straw, or evergreen branches are better. Remember that the plants need air as well as protection.

During mild weather, attend to tree pruning. Shrub

pruning can also be done with advantage. Make sure that your tools are sharp for this job, and be sure you know what you are pruning and why you make every cut. Don't prune spring-flowering shrubs more than necessary. To do so reduces unduly the amount of spring bloom. Make sure that climbing roses, wisterias, espalier fruit trees, raspberry canes, etc., are securely tied to their support. If they whip back and forth in winter storms, they may be seriously injured. Don't walk across the lawn in winter if you can help it. To do so has an injurious effect on the grasses. Place barriers across places if people are likely to take short cuts. This is a good time to catch up on garden reading. Send to your State Agricultural Experiment Station for bulletins on subjects of special interest.

In West Coast gardens prune grape vines. Dig dahlias and store them. This is a good tree and shrub planting time. In California continue to plant a variety of vegetables. Make sure the soil does not become dry. Irrigate when necessary. Good gardens cannot be grown without adequate water supplies.

In the South December is a fine month for transplanting nearly all trees and shrubs as well as roses. Plant also asparagus crowns. Sow radishes, rutabagas, spinach, and turnips. In the Far South fertilize vegetable and flower garden crops that are now coming along nicely. Spray to control San Jose scale on apples, peaches, and other trees, and magnolia scale on magnolias. A miscible, oil emulsion appropriately diluted is the insecticide to use against these pests.

In all parts of the country put your garden records into good shape and plan your next year's garden.

How to Combat Insects

✣✣✣

Gardening involves constant warfare against bugs. On the whole, the odds are greatly on your side. Contrary to the view held by many beginners and inexpert gardeners, controlling insects and similar pests is not the almost impossible task it seems.

Oh, you'll never lick the enemy completely! Guerilla warfare you'll engage in practically all the time and periodically you'll stage an all-out campaign. But good gardeners raise good crops every season in spite of bugs. And you can, too, if you'll take the trouble to learn something about the creatures that threaten and if at the proper time you do the right things to check them.

Too late, wrong weapons, and ineffective application are the trio of faults that sabotage many attempts to lick the bugs. It's of little use spraying after elm leaves have been skeletonized by the leaf beetle. Stomach poisons have no effect on sucking insects such as scales. Failure to reach the underside of the leaves with a forceful spray means that the red spider population is scarcely reduced though the tops of the leaves are thoroughly wetted.

Be observant. Be curious. Poke among your plants pretty often. Look at their stems. Inspect the under as well as the upper sides of their leaves. Watch out for the first signs of insect trouble. Diagnose and do something.

Send to your State Agricultural Experiment Station for

An insect—the eastern spruce gall aphid—causes these pineapple-like swellings at the bases of young shoots.

European pine-shoot moth larvae feed inside young shoots. Spray afflicted parts with arsenate of lead.

bulletins dealing with insect control, particularly with the control of pests known to infest the kinds of plants you grow.

Diagnosis. Diagnosis is of first importance. A perfectly good control measure may be wasted on the wrong enemy. Don't expect fungicides to kill insects or insecticides to eliminate diseases. If you can't identify the enemy positively send ample samples of the insect or of the damage it does to your State Agricultural Experiment Station for diagnosis.

Most insects and other small animal pests are large enough to be seen with the naked eye, but not all. Nematodes and some mites are microscopic and ordinarily make themselves known only by the damage they do. Others, red spider mites for example, are so small that they can only be seen with difficulty. Yet others work in parts of the plant where they are not seen or hide themselves during daylight hours. Among these are Japanese beetle grubs, black vine weevils, and slugs.

A few insects such as borers, leaf miners and nematodes spend most of their lives inside the actual tissues of the plant. These are difficult or impossible to kill once established. The trick is to exterminate them during that brief part of their life cycle that they spend outside the living plant and to deny them entrance.

Most insects live on the outside of the plant and may be exterminated by dusts, sprays, baits, and similar means.

How They Are Killed. Bugs fall into two groups. Those that feed by chewing and those that feed by sucking. The kind of spray or dust successful against one group will not necessarily kill the other.

Chewing insects are usually most easily eliminated by means of stomach poisons. Sevin is one of the most useful. The idea is to spread the poison on the plant as a dust or spray so that the creature eats it and dies.

Sucking insects will not oblige by eating poisons spread before them. They insert their proboscises beneath the

Dusting can achieve good control of some pests—but consult state or county agencies for safety's sake.

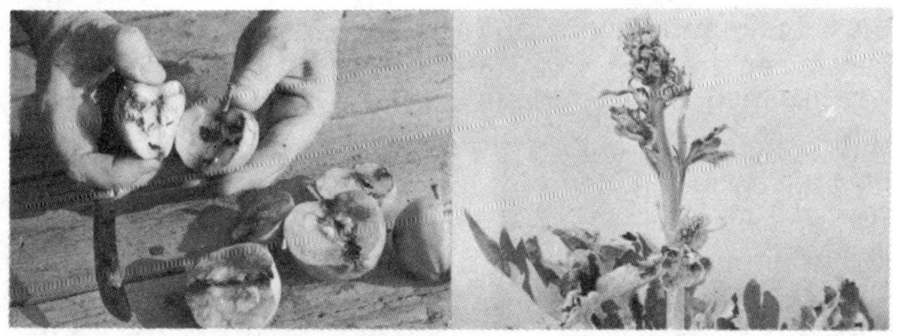

The apple maggot feeds inside the fruit *(photo at left)*. *Right*—a delphinium that has been distorted by mites.

surface skin of the plant and draw into themselves its nutrient juices.

To eliminate suckers use an insecticide that destroys their bodies upon contact. Nicotine, rotenone, pyrethrum, and malathion are standard for this purpose. When using these it is necessary to actually hit the bugs with the spray or dust.

Sprays and Dusts to Use. Some gardeners refuse to spray or dust. They claim that good cultural practices eliminate the need. Rarely is this entirely true. However, the amount of spraying required may be reduced by careful attention to other cultural details. The best plan is to do no more spraying or dusting than is actually necessary, and to use only materials which have no residual (long lasting) effects, and are not suspected of being harmful to humans, when used as directed.

Following World War II excessive zeal developed for the employment of materials, such as DDT, touted to be near miracle workers, in agriculture and horticulture. Some of these, including DDT, proved to have obvious side effects so serious that they adversely affected the well-being of humans. Such materials are not to be trifled with. Their use is now either prohibited or is permitted only under strict controls. Such materials are not for home gardeners. In your spray program stick to such tried and true (and if used properly, harmless) materials as nicotine, sulphur, rotenone, pyrethrum, and any other kinds that have the full stamp of approval of governmental agricultural agencies. Consult your local County Agricultural Agent about which are safe.

Chewing Insects: Beetles and Grubs. The larvae of beetles are grubs (such as Japanese beetle grubs and wireworms) that feed on the roots of plants or bore into their stems (Azalea borer and iris borer). Use Sevin against the mature insects. Control borers by cutting them out or by injecting nicotine paste or other insecticide into their freshly made tunnels or by spraying to prevent entry. Grub-

Tent caterpillar nest.

Mealy bugs gather under leaves, branches.

Mossy rose gall—caused by rose gall wasp sting.

proof lawns and other infected soil areas with preparations recommended by State Agricultural Experiment Stations and sold by dealers for that purpose.

Caterpillars and Cutworms. The larvae of butterflies, moths, and sawflies. Control by hand picking (especially effective with bagworms, tent caterpillers, and web worms which occupy communal "nests"), by applying Sevin or rotenone (non-poisonous) at the first sign of injury. Protect your plants from cut worms by placing paper collars around them or poison the worms with special baits.

Snails and Slugs. Not technically insects. The use of special baits, hand picking (go out at night time with a flashlight. Drop the catch into a receptacle containing brine or kerosene), and sanitation are the best controls. Remove all dead leaves, stones, planks, and other debris that affords daytime hiding places. Keep weeds out.

Sucking Insects: Plant Lice. (Aphids) are soft bodied insects that live in colonies. Spray with malathion, nicotine, or rotenone. For root aphids mix tobacco dust with or spread it on the surface of the soil.

Mealy Bugs are covered with a waxy, mealy substance. Remove by washing with forceful stream of water. Also spray with malathion or nicotine insecticides.

Thrips. Tiny, quick-moving, slender insects which rasp the tissues of the plant and suck its juices. Use methoxychlor.

Scales have hard shells. They move only when extremely small then anchor for life and suck food from the plant. Strong dormant-strength oil or lime-sulphur sprays applied before new leaves come out are effective. So is parathion. Use malathion or nicotine in summer when the young scales move.

Red Spider Mites are not true insects. They are tiny and cause damage and discoloration by sucking on the undersides of the leaves of a great variety of plants. Frequent forceful spraying with clear water is beneficial. Spraying with Kelthane gives excellent control. Nicotine insecticides are also effective.

Lacebugs have transparent wings and work on the undersides of the leaves of rhododendrons, andromedas, azaleas, cotoneasters, etc. Leaf hoppers suck juices from the undersides of the leaves of roses, vines and other plants and hop and fly when disturbed. Tarnished plant bugs cause distortion of the terminal shoots of asters and other plants. These and other sucking pests may attack your plants. Contact insecticides such as malathion and nicotine forcefully applied and repeated will control them.

Fight That Blight

Like animals and humans, plants suffer from diseases caused by infection. Bacteria, fungi, and similar low organisms live and multiply within and upon them. These weaken the plants or bring about their death. To garden well you must control diseases.

The causes of plant diseases are often microscopic. Not always can they be seen by the unaided eye. But they produce symptoms—changes in the appearance of the plant—that are clearly visible.

Unfortunately, the symptoms of one disease may closely resemble those of another. Yet the two may require different treatment. Even more important—symptoms of conditions not caused by disease organisms may look like those of parasitic infections. Spray injury or sun-scorch may resemble leaf spot diseases for example. Yellowing of foliage caused by faulty culture may look like that caused by virus diseases.

Diagnosis is a tricky business. In difficult cases you must leave it to the expert—to the plant pathologist equipped with miscroscope and other tools of science and with a deep knowledge of his subject. Fortunately, the services of such experts are available to you at your State Agricultural Experiment Station and at such institutions as botanical gardens. If you suspect a disease and cannot identify it with certainty, send adequate specimens of the injured plant together with a clear statement of your observations and of the cultural treatment that the plant has received to one of these experts.

You may feel that this wastes precious time. In a few instances it may, but in most cases by the time symptoms are clearly seen by a person unacquainted with the particular disease it is too late to do much to prevent damage during the current season anyway. Treatments for the future may be in order.

The great secret of most successful disease control is prevention rather than cure. To prevent you must know what measures to take and when to take them.

Fortunately the diseases that attack most garden plants are well known and for most, good controls have been worked out. The chief control measures are:

(1) *Good Culture.* Plants grown in unsuitable soils, unsatisfactory locations, or under other unfavorable cultural conditions are less able to resist certain diseases than are those in better environments.

(2) *Sanitation.* This reduces sources of infection. It includes propagation from and the planting of healthy stock only, pruning, picking off, and burning all diseased plant parts, and keeping down weeds.

(3) *Selection of Resistant Varieties.* In a few cases special disease resistant varieties, such as rust-resistant snapdragons and wilt-resistant asters, are available. Use these if the diseases mentioned are prevalent in your locality.

(4) *Disinfection.* Disinfection of the soil with DD, choropicrin, or other fumigant is sometimes necessary for diseases such as sclerotium crown rot.

(5) *Use of Fungicides as Sprays or Dusts.* The most common fungicides are those like Bordeaux mixture in which the killing agent is a form of copper and those, like lime sulphur, in which the killing agent is sulphur. In addition mercuric compounds are used as well as some synthetics.

Symptoms of Diseases. *Leaf Spots* are characteristic of many plant diseases. One of the most serious is black spot of roses. Delphinium black spot is another, fungus leaf spot of chrysanthemum yet a third. Once the spots show on a leaf that particular leaf cannot be cured because the disease organism is working inside its tissues. Wherever possible pick off and burn affected leaves and spray or dust repeatedly (usually at about weekly intervals) to keep unaffected and newly developing leaves constantly covered with a protective film of fungicide. Bordeaux mixture, sulphur dusts, and fermate are effective. In fall burn all dead leaves and stems. With roses and other plants known to suffer from leaf spot diseases don't wait until the spots show before beginning treatment. Beat the disease to the punch. Start spraying or dusting early in the season and keep it up.

Mildews. Mildews appear on leaves as white felty coverings. They are common on lilacs, roses, phlox, and many other plants. Moist atmospheric conditions and poor air circulation favor their development. Dusting with sulphur gives adequate control.

Rusts. Not every condition that causes a rusty appearance of foliage and stems is a true rust disease. Best known of the rusts are those that infect snapdragons and hollyhocks causing small reddish, orange, or brown pustules to develop and the cedar-apple rust which spends part of its life on Eastern red-cedar (*Juniperus virginiana*) and part on apple, hawthorn or quince trees. On the cedar it causes galls as big as marbles, on the alternate hosts conspicuous yellow spots. Get rust resistant strains of snapdragon. Dust hollyhocks regularly with sulphur. Avoid growing red-cedars near apples and other alternate hosts, or pick the galls off cedars, and spray the alternate hosts with Bordeaux mixture as the leaves are developing.

Cankers are characterized by the shrinking or enlargement and the cracking and dying of stems. They are most prevalent on woody plants such as roses, pears, and apples. Cut out and burn the affected parts. Use fungicides, too.

Galls, roundish swellings on leaves, branches, or roots may be caused by insects, nematodes, and other agencies besides infectious diseases. Some disease-produced galls, such as crown-gall of roses and other plants, are serious. Cut the galls out and burn them. If plants are removed, sterilize the soil before replanting. Spraying with Bordeaux mixture is effective sometimes, as for azalea gall.

Blights kill young stems, foliage, and other tissues. The symptoms usually begin at the tips of shoots and extend downwards, but not always. Petal blight of azaleas attacks the flowers. One of the commonest is Botrytis blight which attacks peonies and other plants causing a gray mold to appear on them. Peony and rose buds often fail to open because of it. Another Botrytis blight is common on tulips. Control these particular blights by strict sanitation—picking off and burning affected parts and by spraying repeatedly with botran or Bordeaux mixture during spring. Other blights need other treatments.

Wilts. Wilts caused by disease are rarely curable once the symptoms (flabbiness or drooping of leaves and stems) are visible. Remove and burn affected plants. Sterilization of the soil may be necessary. Wilt-resistant varieties of aster are available. Wilting (the symptoms) can result from other causes.

Rots result in the rapid breaking down and decay (often into foul-smelling masses) of plant tissues. Crown rot of delphinium (which also affects many other plants) and soft rot of irises are common examples. Controls are based on removal and burning of affected parts, upon not setting plants subject to infection in the same ground unless it is first sterilized and, in the case of iris, upon eliminating borers which spread the disease. Disinfection of the plants before setting and of all tools used on infected plants is important.

Damping Off refers to destruction of seedlings by fungi that cause them to die at the soil line and topple over. Sterilization of the soil and proper cultural care in such matters as providing good drainage, reasonable air circulation, and care in watering give effective control.

Viruses. Virus diseases cause much distress. Mosaic disease of dahlias causes mottling of the leaves and stunting. Aster yellow causes discoloration and distortion of growth of asters and other plants. Plants affected with virus diseases cannot be cured. Destroy plants as soon as discovered. Protect by eliminating insects, and other pests that carry the disease.

Weeding

Weeds are less difficult to control than many people think. Systematize your attempts to eradicate them and you can have a clean garden with minimum effort.

Don't misunderstand me. I have no magic formula to offer. The most recent scientific advances in the use of herbicides (a fancy name for weed-killers) do not make weeding workless. But by using your head and modern methods you can save a good deal of tiresome chore-work.

What's wrong with weeds anyway? Why bother about a few plant-volunteers some of which, like dandelions and chicory, have pretty nice-looking flowers?

In the first place weeds give an untidy appearance to a garden. Secondly, they reduce crop yields and harm plantings by taking food, moisture, and light that are needed by cultivated plants, and thirdly they act as hosts and sources of infection for diseases and pests. There are other disadvantages but these are the main ones.

Weeds are an extravagance. You just can't afford to have them. They make your gardening efforts ineffective. What's the use of fertilizing, if pigweed luxuriates on the food you provide? Of watering, to give dandelions additional moisture? Of dusting hollyhocks to control rust, when mallow weeds nearby preserve the fungus and spread it with every breeze?

The Weeds. There are, of course, hundreds of kinds of weeds. Whether a plant is considered so may depend upon where it is as well as upon what it is.

Dandelion is a crop in the vegetable garden; in lawn it's a weed. Clover may be cultivated in the lawn but is a weed in the vegetable garden. In the path both dandelion and clover are weeds.

All weeds are either annuals (for practical purposes the few that are technically biennials may be included here) or perennials. The former must renew themselves each year from seeds. The latter persist for many years.

Control of annual weeds is based upon destroying them before they set seeds. If this is done, ground will be free of such weeds the following year except for those that spring from seeds brought in by the wind, on the shoes, in manure and in other ways.

In practice, some such weed seeds always are brought in, therefore you must fight annual weeds each year. Nevertheless, early destruction of every annual weed before it seeds, must be the keystone of your control program. Don't limit the prevention of seeding to the weeds actually in your garden. If possible, apply it to the surrounding areas also.

Prevention of seeding is also important with perennial weeds. It destroys one method by which they propagate themselves. But of itself it is not sufficient to eliminate weed specimens already established in your garden. In many cases these spread by vegetative means and may rapidly take over considerable areas.

One thing to bear in mind is this. Any plant can be killed by preventing it for long enough from forming leaves. Even the vilest weed dies as a result of this treatment. Therefore hoe early and often.

Methods of Control. To keep weeds down you will use some (or all) of the following methods (1) hand pulling (2) hoeing or cultivating (3) digging (4) smothering (5) fertilization (6) weed killers.

Select methods of control not only with reference to the

kind of weeds you are combatting but also to where they are growing.

In the Lawn. Believe it or not the surest way to keep your lawn weed-free is to grow good grass. Healthy, vigorous lawn grasses don't give weed seedlings a chance. They smother out established weeds. Anything you can do to promote luxuriant grass reduces your weed problem.

In the first place prepare a deep, weed-free, extremely fertile seed bed for the grass (see chapter on "The Lawn"). A weed-free bed is obtained by carefully digging out perennial weeds, by preparing the area some weeks (in extreme cases even months) in advance of sowing, and by, in the interim, repeatedly cultivating the surface shallowly to destroy annuals before they seed, and perennials before their leaves or stems are more than an inch high.

Sow only the best quality grass seed. Cheap mixtures often contain high proportions of weed seeds. Sow at the most favorable time of the year. Hand-pull any weed seedlings that appear as early as possible.

Fertilize in spring and early fall (but not in summer), water when needed, don't cut the grass too short. In every other way encourage good grass.

Even so, you may find a few weeds invading your lawn. Get after them early. Don't let them establish a beachhead.

Hand pulling, or digging out, if necessary, to remove deep rooted kinds, is still effective where the area is not extraordinarily large—and even then it helps. Selective sprays such as those containing the chemical 2,4D eliminate broad leaved weeds such as dandelions and plantains without permanently harming the grasses, and some success has been obtained in the use of selective weed killers on crab grass (which is narrow-leaved). When using these be especially careful to follow strictly the manufacturer's directions. Take the utmost care that none of the spray drifts, even in very slight amounts, on to trees, shrubbery, or other plants that you don't want harmed.

These chemicals are exceedingly potent. Wash spraying equipment out very thoroughly after their use or, better still, keep one piece of equipment for their use only.

In the Vegetable Garden, Flower Garden, and Similar Cultivated Areas: The hoe or cultivator still are the most effective tools for destroying weeds between rows and between plants spaced widely enough to allow working space. Supreme among these for the small garden is the scuffle (or Dutch) hoe. In using this most effective instrument push it back and forth so that its blade cuts through the soil not more than an inch beneath the surface. Do not lift it off the ground at the end of the stroke. Work backwards so that you do not step upon the hoed ground.

If weeds have gotten a little ahead and are too stubborn to be eradicated with the Dutch hoe use a regular chop hoe. Cultivators of the Planet Junior type are excellent between rows in larger gardens.

Which tool you use is less important than how and when you use it. Do not cultivate deeply. To do so destroys roots near the surface. Seize every opportunity when the weather is hot and dry to destroy weeds by cultivating. The effort you expend on such days is two, three, or more times effective than the same effort spent in dull, moist weather.

Cultivation does not destroy weeds in the rows nor is it practicable among plants set very closely together. Then hand weeding must be done. Weeds pull easiest when the ground is fairly moist. Choose such occasions, when you can, for hand weeding. Take care not to disturb the roots of seedlings that the weeds grow near. If you do loosen the soil about them, press it back.

Mulching—that is, spreading a layer of loose compost, peat moss, leaf mold, buckwheat hulls, or the like over the surface of the soil between plants greatly cuts down the weed problem. Even if a few weeds do grow, they tend to root in the mulch and are very easily pulled.

In the Shrub Border: A mulch of compost, straw, manure, leaf mold or similar material is the best solution to the weed problem among shrubbery and this is particularly true where shallow-rooted shrubs such as azaleas are grown. Hoes and cultivators should never be used near them. They can be used among regular deeper rooting shrubs if mulching is not practicable.

Sources of Horticultural Information

Your state agricultural experiment station is one of the best sources of gardening information. Other sources are horticultural societies, garden clubs, gardening departments of newspapers, and botanical gardens. In the list below the names of cities and towns following the names of the states indicate the postal addresses of the agricultural experiment stations. For instance, "Arizona: Tucson" and "Pennsylvania: State College" indicate that correspondence should be addressed to Arizona State Agricultural Experiment Station, Tucson, Ariz., and to Pennsylvania State Agricultural Experiment Station, State College, Pa.

Alabama: Auburn
Alaska: College
Arizona: Tucson
Arkansas: Fayetteville
California: Berkeley
Colorado: Fort Collins
Connecticut: New Haven
Connecticut: Storrs
Delaware: Newark
Florida: Gainesville
Georgia: Coastal Plain Station, Tifton
Hawaii: Honolulu
Idaho: Moscow
Illinois: Urbana
Indiana: Lafayette
Iowa: Ames
Kansas: Manhattan
Kentucky: Lexington
Louisiana: Baton Rouge
Maine: Orono
Maryland: College Park
Massachusetts: Amherst
Michigan: East Lansing
Minnesota: St. Paul
Mississippi: State College
Missouri: College Station, Columbia
Missouri: Fruit Station, Mountain Grove
Missouri: Poultry Station, Mountain Grove
Montana: Bozeman
Nebraska: Lincoln
Nevada: Reno
New Hampshire: Durham
New Jersey: New Brunswick
New Mexico: State College
New York: State Station, Geneva
New York: Cornell Station, Ithaca
North Carolina: Raleigh
North Dakota: Fargo
Ohio: Wooster
Oklahoma: Stillwater
Oregon: Corvallis
Pennsylvania: State College
Puerto Rico: Federal Station, Mayaguez
Puerto Rico: Insular Station, Rio Piedras
Rhode Island: Kingston
South Carolina: Clemson
South Dakota: Brookings
Tennessee: Knoxville
Texas: College Station
Utah: Logan
Vermont: Burlington
Virginia: College Station, Blacksbury
Virginia: Truck Station, Norfolk
Washington: College Station, Pullman
Washington: Western Station, Puyallup
West Virginia: Morgantown
Wisconsin: Madison
Wyoming: Laramie

Index